Immodest
& SENSATIONAL

150 YEARS OF CANADIAN WOMEN IN SPORT

Immodest & SENSATIONAL

150 YEARS OF CANADIAN WOMEN IN SPORT

M. ANN HALL

James Lorimer & Company Ltd., Publishers
Toronto

James Lorimer & Company Ltd., Publishers acknowledge the support of the Ontario Arts Council. We acknowledge the support of the Government of Canada through the Book Publishing Industry Development Program (BPIDP) for our publishing activities. We acknowledge the support of the Canada Council for the Arts for our publishing program. We acknowledge the support of the Government of Ontario through the Ontario Media Development Corporation's Ontario Book Initiative.

Library and Archives Canada Cataloguing in Publication

Hall, M. Ann (Margaret Ann), 1942–
    Immodest and sensational : 150 years of Canadian women in sport / M. Ann Hall.

Includes index.
ISBN 978-1-55277-021-4 (pbk.)

    1. Women athletes—Canada—Biography. 2. Sports for women—Canada—History.
3. Women sportswriters—Canada—Biography. I. Title.
GV697.A1H35 2008   796'.082092271   C2008-903402-3

James Lorimer & Company Ltd., Publishers
317 Adelaide Street West, Suite 1002
Toronto, Ontario
M5V 1P9
www.lorimer.ca

Printed in China

Contents

Introduction   7
1 Cycling to Emancipation   12
2 Modern Mannish Maidens   19
3 Girls' Sport Run by Girls   31
4 Pushing the Boundaries   43
5 Sweetheart Heroines   51
6 Favourite Daughters and Competing Mothers   59
7 Unrecognized Champions and Media Darlings   69
8 Fighting for Gender Equality   79
Epilogue   87

Notable Firsts and Achievements in Canadian Women's Sport   89
Where to Find More Information about Canada's Athletic Heroines   91
Further Reading   93
Acknowledgements   94
Illustration Credits   94
Index   95

A skating carnival at Victoria Rink in Montreal, 1870, from a composite of photographs taken by William Notman and then painted in oil.

INTRODUCTION

In 1879, six young ladies in Ottawa wrote to the local newspaper issuing a challenge to women in nearby Prescott to a game of football, the prize being a silver cup. The newspaper gave their request publicity, but added: "we do not think there are any young ladies in Prescott who are ambitious to become champion kickers." The same year, at the Dominion Day Regatta at Lorne Park in Ontario, a race was listed on the program: "Ladies Race — half mile straight-away; to be rowed in eighteen-feet inrigged lap-streak boats. Open to all ladies — prize to be a handsome gold ring." Scattered references like these attesting to those who challenged Victorian notions of female propriety by engaging in unusual activities are all that remain of an earlier era.

One of the earliest known sport clubs for women in Canada was the Montreal Ladies Archery Club, formed in 1858. It had its own practice ground on St. Catherine Street and held regular meetings and annual competitions with prizes. Women also formed their own snowshoe clubs, such as the Ladies' Prince of Wales Club of Montreal, founded in 1861; on the odd occasion, men's clubs would arrange short tramps or races for them, but they were usually banned from the longer male-only tramps and confined to the welcoming party at the evening's social event.

Very limited forms of physical activity were available to Canadian women in the 1860s and 1870s, and those considered appropriate were individual or family recreations, restricted mostly to those of wealth and leisure. Young women in this position were never at a loss for entertainment; there were sleigh and toboggan parties, ice-boating, skating balls and ice carnivals in winter, and picnics, croquet, boating and fishing excursions in summer.

Ice skating was by far the most popular winter activity, especially after the advent of heated covered rinks brightened by gas lamps. Fancy skating and the ability to trace artistic patterns on the ice, the forerunner of figure skating, became popular; so too did skating carnivals and fancy-dress balls. A few enthusiasts tried roller skating, or "parlour"

Two women on snowshoes in 1866, from a water-colour by Capt. Francis G. Coleridge, who was stationed at the British garrison in Montreal.

Women and girls swimming at Murray Bay in Charlevoix, Quebec, in 1871.

The warm blanket coat was often worn by women to go snowshoeing, skating or tobogganing.

skating, in summer on the floor-covered rinks. Horseback riding remained a popular outdoor diversion in summer, and more women took part in fox hunting. Riding habits were probably the first sportswear sold in Canada for women, along with bathing costumes, which took yards of material to make certain all flesh was appropriately covered. Lady tobogganists were advised never to wear hoops; some enthusiasts solved the problem by removing their crinolines and wrapping themselves in a sheet as they careened down the hill. A distinct improvement on sheets were the warm blanket coats with red epaulets and sashes, pointed hoods, sealskin turbans and moccasins that later became the favoured apparel.

In the 1870s, walking matches, or pedestrianism, became the rage, but more as spectacle than mass sport. A few brave souls entered special women's races like the one at

Men, women and children tobogganing and sledding near Montreal circa 1850.

Perry's Hall in Montreal early in 1879. The two contestants were Miss L.A. Warren from Philadelphia and Miss Jessie Anderson of Montreal, both eighteen years old. The distance was 25 miles, monotonously round and round on a narrow track in a small hall with stifling ventilation, made worse by "smoking and expectorating." Miss Warren collapsed suddenly after 21 miles, allowing Miss Anderson to continue walking without competition, finishing in 5 hours and 21 ½ minutes amidst "great enthusiasm." Her prize was a handsome gold hunting case watch.

Despite the circus atmosphere, side-betting and unruly spectators, another walking match took place later the same year, also in Montreal but this time in the roller skating rink. There were three contestants: Miss Jessie Morahan of Montreal, Miss Edwards of New York and Miss Kilberry from Boston. The race lasted two days: the contestants walked round and round the rink, starting early in the morning and finishing late at night. Spectators came and went, and the building was filled with music to make the spectacle more attractive and to help the women accomplish their task. Each was dressed in an ankle- or knee-length black satin dress, but interestingly what they wore on their feet is unknown. A newspaper report characterized Miss Morahan as a brunette, somewhat "heavy featured," decidedly Amazonian in proportions, and with the countenance and bearing of a professional athlete. The winner (Miss Edwards) walked a total of 80 miles, and the Canadian walker came third, having accomplished 60 miles. The pedestrianism craze lasted not much longer than a decade due to social pressure from temperance officials, religious conservatives and many medical doctors who branded this form of women's sporting entertainment both cruel and immoral.

Long before the first European women settled in Canada in the early seventeenth century, Native women worked and played in the various hunting and gathering, fishing and farming cultures of early Aboriginal peoples, including the Inuit groups in the North, the Iroquoian and Algonquian peoples in the East, the Plains Indians of the prairies and several distinct tribes along the Pacific coast. We know little about women's lives in these early Native societies, especially before the coming of the Europeans, but we do know that among their amusements and leisure were many indigenous games and contests, activities we today call sports, like shinny, lacrosse and foot-

ball. Some games were restricted to men, some to women, and in a few both sexes participated, sometimes against each other.

Shinny, a hockey-like ball game played on a field or on ice in winter, was often considered a women's game. The small round ball, made of wood or stuffed buckskin, was hit along the ground (or ice) by a curved stick; the object was to get it through two posts or sticks at either end of the field. Double ball, a more difficult and faster version of shinny, was also primarily a women's game. Two balls were tied together with a thong and tossed about using a long, slender stick.

Baggaa'atowe (as the Ojibwa called it), or lacrosse (as the Jesuits named it), was mainly a men's game, often with religious and ceremonial significance, and was used as a training exercise for young warriors. Among some tribes, women would run out onto the field and bestow gifts of beads or other tokens to their favourite player, causing George Beers, a Montreal dentist who in the late nineteenth century modified and organized lacrosse for white players, to comment: "… if Canada's fair daughters would revive the fashion! How it would put one on one's mettle to be a crack player!" Some tribes permitted women to play providing it was away from male eyes, but in a few the two sexes played together and the women were allowed to touch the ball with their hands.

Double ball was one of many traditional sports and games played by Aboriginal women.

Shoshonie women from the northwest Plains were adept at throwing the lasso from horseback.

Most football-type games were like modern-day soccer, where a ball (often of stuffed deer hide) was kicked between two goal posts. When men and women played together, the women could often throw the ball whereas the men had to kick it — an early example of games being modified for females.

Many Native women's traditions — certainly their earlier games and amusements — most likely continued in some modified form, but there was little space for them in the white women's world. Regardless, their games and sports did not disappear once they were gradually resettled on Native reserves; we just know very little about them. Unlike several Native male runners and lacrosse teams, who often toured with their own shows for the entertainment of colonial settlers, nineteenth-century Aboriginal women rarely participated in any form of white-organized sport. One exception appears to be water regattas, where Native women sometimes took part in canoeing events. On one such occasion in 1867, Montreal's *Gazette* reported that in a race for Native women, two war canoes "each manned or rather womanned by six or eight squaws . . . came forward to battle for aqueous supremacy." The unflattering account described them as hefty women, each dressed in "modest skirts and jacket of crimson, orange or unassuming blue, each jabbering with female loquacity."

Most were reluctant, many more were completely diffident, yet some young Canadian women were determined to prove that sports were for everyone, not just the few brave souls willing to risk their reputations and endure the inevitable public criticism. They wanted to become athletes just like their brothers. This is their story.

Chapter One

CYCLING TO EMANCIPATION

Billed as the "champion female bicycle rider of the world," Louise Armaindo (whose real name was Brisbois), from Ste-Clet, near Montreal, was willing to race against men, women and, if need be, horses. Women's bicycle racing was a popular spectator sport in the last decades of the nineteenth century, and Louise was one of several stars to emerge who entertained large and supportive crowds throughout the United States and eastern Canada. Riding a high-wheeler, a Yale model with a 51-inch front wheel, a small back one, solid rubber tires and highly perched seat, she challenged any woman to a race. She also challenged any man, providing he gave her a 2-mile head start in a 20-mile race and 5 miles in a 50-mile race. She would invariably beat the women and sometimes the men.

Dressed in a short crimson jacket trimmed with silver lace, a diamond crescent glittering at her throat, red trunks and white stockings topped with a red silk cap, she was accused of "scanty attire," yet often found herself too heavily clad for such arduous exercise. One of her specialities was the 6-day race where competitors raced on an indoor track for 8 hours a day, usually from 3 p.m. to 6 p.m. and then from 8 p.m. until 1 a.m., for 6 days continuously. Since a percentage of the gate receipts was divided among the winners, it was important to attract as many spectators as possible. At the world championship for women held at New York's Madison Square Garden in 1889, some 3,000 spectators daily watched 15 riders each accumulate over 600 miles throughout the 6 days. Louise Armaindo lost that race; in fact she came so far back she didn't win anything, but race officials presented her with $300 anyway. Like circus and variety theatre performers, these women made a living exhibiting their strength and athletic bodies; denounced by some as common show girls, they were in fact highly trained and motivated athletes.

Very few ordinary women rode the high-wheel bicycles because they were difficult to mount,

Louise Armaindo, from a lithograph published in The National Police Gazette *on May 10, 1884.*

especially with long skirts, and dangerous once you were up. Athletic young men in military-style uniforms joined bicycle clubs, which organized race meets, riding displays, tours and outings; women were not wanted. Tricycles were a little more accommodating for women — even Queen Victoria thought so proven by her purchase of two in 1881 — and the tandem variety was popular among well-off couples.

By the mid-1880s smaller, lighter bicycles with equal-size wheels driven by a sprocket and chain began to appear on the scene. At first the tires were of hard rubber and glued to the rim, but they were quickly superseded by the pneumatic tire, at last making the bicycle safe, comfortable and attractive to everyone, including women. The first appearance in a town or city of a "lady cyclist" was often reported in the local newspaper. The following note in the St. John's *Daily News* in Newfoundland was typical: "A spectacle of an unusual and sensational character was for the first time witnessed in the city on Gower Street last evening, a young lady bicycling with all the ease and dignity of a professional."

The high-wheeler soon faded from the scene to become the favourite prop of clowns and vaude-villians; at the same time, bicycle clubs of a different nature, more social than fraternal, began to sprout up all over the country. Relatively well-off women with the means to purchase a new "safety" bicycle (they sold for $50 to $110) flocked to these clubs. By 1895, there were some 10,000 "wheelmen and wheelwomen" in Toronto, and the popular Knickerbocker Club, open to both sexes, was inundated with applications for membership from those wishing to take part in summer jaunts of a "purely social character." In Winnipeg, the exclusively female Tam O'Shanter

Top: A Comet high-wheeler, or penny farthing, bicycle manufactured in Ontario in 1887.
Bottom: A group of cyclists in Alymer, Quebec, embarking on a summer outing on the latest pneumatic tire "safeties" circa 1898.

A studio photo of W.K. Masterman and lady on a tandem bicycle, taken by Wm. Notman & Son in Montreal in 1896.

Club enhanced its popularity by inviting gentlemen to accompany the members on outings, and "whatever little gathering takes place after the run is entirely at the expense of the ladies."

As clubs were deluged with female members, they often decided to form a branch of their own. The bicycle offered women, at least those who could afford one and had the time to enjoy it, a means to encourage exercise and good health, entertainment, transportation and, above all, freedom. They were now free to go where they wanted, when they wanted and with whom they wanted without a chaperone. Only a horse had offered this sort of independence, but a bicycle, or "silent steed," was a good deal cheaper, travelled faster and further, and did not have to be fed, watered or bedded down at night.

Although it was possible for women in long skirts to ride a safety bicycle, especially if they put lead sinkers in their hems and guards over the back wheels to keep their skirts out of the spokes, they were more inclined to adopt shorter styles, including the controversial bloomers with tight-fitting, knee-length hose, or the more acceptable split skirt. The bloomer costume had been worn at mid-century by the prominent American writer, lecturer and champion of women's rights, Amelia Bloomer, who wore it to defy tradition and cope with muddy streets. She had met with such vociferous criticism that the fashion soon quietly faded into obscurity — only to be revived again some forty years later with the advent of the safety bicycle, along with the controversy. The front page of *The Halifax Herald* on October 1, 1895, invited readers to "judge for yourself which costume is most becoming" by printing a large cutout of both Queen Victoria and Mrs. Cleveland (wife of the United States president) where it was possible to fold the paper and show these women wearing either a skirt or a bloomer costume.

Not all public opinion was unfavourable. When girls and women on bicycles in small-town Petrolia, Ontario, took to wearing huge bloomers and hose, the local paper applauded and called the elderly ladies and gentlemen who decried the new fashion "sanctimonious hypocrites," at the same time issuing an angry blast against the "low remarks of rude and ignorant loafers." As the Toronto *Globe* pointed out, "one bicyclist wearing an advanced costume does more towards furthering dress reform than a score of theorists, writers and lecturers."

Many women would not wear the contentious bloomers, and instead adopted a daring but practical split skirt, which became known appropriately as the "bicycle skirt." Three-piece "Ladies' Bicycle Suits," comprising a Norfolk jacket, skirt and bloomers, made of navy blue all-wool serge, sold for $15 dollars. The well-turned-out cyclist, wrote one commentator, should wear a neatly cut, ankle-length skirt with spats to match, knickerbockers of the same material, a small Eton coat fitted to the waist, gloves of white chamois leather, topped by a tam-o'-shanter hat. Another enthusiast suggested that black, navy and light brown were the best colours, with the latter being the most serviceable because it did not show the dust.

An ad from the height of the bicycle craze.

Unwary pedestrians soon found city streets a hazardous place to walk, and the plea went out to all cyclists, especially female ones, to "learn before you venture in the streets and so run the risk of endangering not only your own lives but ours too." Special bicycle schools were opened by innovative entrepreneurs who saw the potential to make some money in empty indoor skating rinks during the spring and summer months, and by bicycle companies hoping to sell their product to newly trained graduates. In Toronto, the Remington Cycle School at McDonald & Willson's bicycle store on Yonge Street opened in March 1896 in a well-lit hall with sufficient room to allow several riders to use the floor at the same time. Women riders were taught how to stay upright and, most importantly, "the correct movement of the ankle which makes all the difference between a graceful and ungraceful rider."

Not long after, two more large riding academies appeared in Toronto: H.A. Lozier & Co., manufacturers of the Cleveland wheel, opened their hall at the Granite rink, free from any impediments such as posts; and the Hyslop school, located on King Street, boasted a long stretch on either side of its hall so that the beginner did not have to turn.

The benefits and dangers of cycling by women were the cause of much debate in the 1890s among medical practitioners, both male and female. An editorial in *The Dominion Medical Monthly and Ontario Medical Journal* laid out the grounds of the debate quite simply — either bicycle riding was good for women, or it was

Cycling clubs, such as this one in Ottawa, Ontario, became very popular, especially in the 1890s.

"injurious and should not be tolerated." There were two reasons why someone might believe the latter. One was on the grounds of "propriety," and even the writer of the editorial acknowledged that medical doctors should have little to say about matters of opinion and custom. The second reason, far more serious, was that cycling was "injurious to the rider herself and decidedly immoral in its tendencies." The saddle was not suited to female anatomy, the uterus would be seriously jolted, and "pelvic mischief" would befall the poor woman who rode during her menstrual period. Very few of these claims were supported by medical research and evidence, and Canadian medical journals often simply reprinted editorials from their British and American counterparts.

Women doctors, far fewer in numbers then their male counterparts, also entered the cycling debates, and were usually cautiously supportive. Elizabeth Mitchell and Grace Ritchie, in a lively session about the rise and merits of female athleticism at the 1896 annual meeting of the National Council of Women of Canada, praised the bicycle for its role in dress reform and in countering negative attitudes towards women taking up exercise in general. "We should have recreation in the form of exercise, or athleticism as a duty from the good it will do us physically and morally and mentally," commented Dr. Ritchie to enthusiastic audience applause. American Lucy Hall, both a physician and a cycling enthusiast, admonished male doctors who suggested that women would do as well to run a sewing machine as to ride a bicycle because the motion was precisely the same. Any woman, she argued, who is physically able to walk is capable of riding a bicycle; she also urged that "the timid as well as the more self-confident women should take it up quietly, but freely and persistently." Others pointed to the inconsistency of condemning women who rode in the open air for a short time while saying nothing about women running sewing machines in hot, stuffy rooms for hours on end.

Not all women agreed with this philosophy,

Two well-dressed women cyclists in Nova Scotia circa 1900.

nor were they as supportive. At the height of the bicycle craze in the mid-1890s, the Women's Rescue League in the United States announced a national crusade against the use of bicycles by women. They circulated a strongly worded petition, aimed at Congress, linking the riding of bicycles, more than any other medium, to the swelling ranks of "fallen" and "reckless" girls in the United States. Their circular denounced bicycle riding by young women because it produced "an immoral association in both language and dress, which have a tendency to make women not only unwomanly, but immodest as well."

Toronto journalist C.S. Clark, in his famous tract *Of Toronto the Good* (1898) exposing the supposed "social evil" of his beloved "Queen City," noted the Women's Rescue League petition and made his own observations: "A girl would be considered decidedly immodest did she go on long [snowshoe] tramps with boys, but on her bicycle she can at the same time gratify her taste for boys' society and satisfy the demands of propriety, which takes cognizance not so much of what you do, but how you do it, and questions your motives not at all." Clark was far more concerned about the corruption of boys and young

Advertising art evoking the exhilarating freedom the bicycle offered the modern young woman, depicted here in the new bloomer costume.

men than he was about young women: "I assert that one girl in a bloomer costume will create far greater and more widespread corruption among boys than a city full of show bills, so will a well developed girl in short dresses." Trustees of the Toronto Board of Education must have agreed with him because they instructed their inspectors to report "the names of all female teachers who have been riding bicycles in male attire, commonly called 'bloomers.'"

A woman riding a bicycle in the 1890s was the embodiment of the New Woman, the one leaving behind the fragile stereotype of her earlier, domestic sister and marching determinedly towards more education, work, service and suffrage. These same women were generally young, middle-class,

and often did not have to work to support themselves. It is misleading to imagine that all middle-class women in late Victorian Canada experienced a metamorphosis and emerged dramatically as "new" women, because there were powerful forces in society making certain they were not too different from the generations who had preceded them. An ideology of separate spheres, promoted by clergymen, physicians, educators and lawmakers, meant a sharp distinction between the domestic world of women and the public world of men. The very real threat represented by the bicycle was that it would remove women from the home, along with its familial obligations and moral insulation. "Though all women become wheelers," assured one woman cycling enthusiast, "they yet will remain women, and as wives and mothers they will preserve the order of households and by precept and example purify and elevate family life."

Before the bicycle, more and more women in Canada, at least those who could afford the costs and had the time, began to participate in a variety of sports, from skating and tobogganing in winter to swimming, equestrianism, croquet, tennis and golf in summer. But these activities did not acquire anything resembling a mass appeal. What was needed was an easily learned, enjoyable, outdoor exercise that was robust and healthy yet did not breach late nineteenth-century standards of proper decorum. Cycling met these conditions.

As the last decade of the nineteenth century came to a close, Victorian women rode their bicycles to physical emancipation and dress reform, forever changing the look and style of women's sport in Canada. As one historian observed, the bicycle extended "her sphere across the threshold, for in loosening her stays and dividing her skirts, the New Woman also took possession of her own movements and achieved a measure of self-confidence that carried her into the twentieth century."

Chapter Two

MODERN MANNISH MAIDENS

The year was 1890. The Toronto *Globe* reprinted a British attack upon "modern mannish maidens" and the craze for mannish sports and ways among young women in polite society. A particular sport or recreation was inappropriate unless it conformed to a test: no girl or woman should be seen playing in public if "she is liable to pose therein ungracefully, clumsily, or unbecoming." Acceptable sports were horsemanship, walking, climbing, rowing, skating, lawn tennis, badminton and golf. Clearly unacceptable were the "manly" sports, team games requiring strength, speed and sometimes physical contact, like cricket, soccer, rugby, grass hockey, rounders (a form of baseball) and their equivalents in Canada — lacrosse, football and baseball. It was also reported that students at Wellesley, a women's college in the United States, were going to take up lacrosse because it was healthy, vigorous and "perfectly dignified." The *Globe* editors were astonished and commented that "there must be a variety of the game that we have not seen in Canada."

Team sports required "violent running" and this was seen as a problem. Those who thought they knew better argued that women were naturally not built to run, their movement constrained and awkward: "A kind of precipitate waddle with neither grace, fitness, nor dignity." While there were many who praised the healthful gains achieved by women through moderate and lady-like forms of exercise, these same enthusiasts, whether they were medical doctors, clergy, educators or physical culturists, warned of the dangers and problems in allowing women to realize their athletic potential. Mild exercise was clearly an antidote to the physical deterioration of young girls, particularly those of the sedentary middle class exposed to new intellectual demands. On the other hand, the rapid emergence of a

Ethel (Hatt) Babbitt won many provincial and Maritime tennis championships before the First World War.

Violet Summerhayes, Canadian tennis champion between 1899 and 1904.

much more robust woman in the last decade of the century threatened a society uncertain of how to adapt to the New Woman and the consequent blurring of traditional gender divisions and roles.

Aside from the supposed danger to a woman's reproductive system, the real threat posed by sport was that it gave the middle-class woman the freedom to leave the home. Relieved of family and domestic responsibilities, she was no longer under the moral guidance of a father or husband. In short, she was able to move back and forth between the private and public spheres. Sport, especially tennis and golf, allowed athletic women of means the opportunity for social interaction and competition.

Tennis was considered an effeminate game by the more manly and rugged team-playing male athletes, which meant that women could play it with impunity. By 1883, a Dominion ladies' championship was in place, but there were rarely enough contestants until 1892, when it became firmly established (today it is called the Rogers Cup). The winner that year was Maude Delano-Osborne from Sutton, Ontario, a young woman with "indomitable perseverance and determination." She held the title until 1895, when she was beaten by Ottawa's Mrs. Sydney Smith (media accounts of the day rarely provided the first names of married women). Dressed in high-necked, ankle-length, white linen dresses cinched at the waist, and with no proper running shoes, women players were not surprisingly more comfortable lobbing "moonballs" — high, floating shots from one side of the baseline to the other. Later that year, Maude and Mrs. Smith travelled to Buffalo to compete in a tournament, to be among the first Canadian women venturing outside Canada to compete in organized sport. Maude Delano-Osborne married and became Mrs. Eustace Smith, the name she competed under after 1895. Two of their daughters, Maude and Cecil, became successful figure skaters.

Canadian championships in those days were restricted to those who could afford to come. The jewel of the summer circuit was held at Niagara-on-the-Lake on the shores of Lake Ontario. Although a tennis tournament, it was also a social occasion for well-heeled ladies and gentlemen who travelled in the same circles. On the women's side, the tournament usually attracted the United States champion who sometimes won, but in 1899, Violet Summerhayes of Toronto unexpectedly beat the American champion. She also beat all comers for the next six years. Who was she? Aside from a name in the record book, we know nothing of her.

Fortunately, we know a little more about Lois

Lois Moyes Bickle, 1907, winner of ten Canadian singles champions and eight doubles championships.

Moyes Bickle, winner of ten Canadian singles championships (the first in 1906), eight times doubles winner (with Florence Best), and the first woman to win both the east and west coast championships. Strong and tall, she was active in other sports like swimming, skating, bowling, squash and badminton. Gardening was also a passion and her horticultural achievements won awards, as did her prize cockerels, raised in the backyard of her Rosedale home in Toronto. As a tennis player she was admired for her smashing serve, tenacity, skill and sportsmanlike conduct. She would also help younger players develop their skills by practising with them. "If Canadian tennis is ever to amount to anything particularly among women," she advised, "our players have got to learn to hit harder."

Another worthy tennis champion was Ethel (Hatt) Babbitt, the first woman inducted into the New Brunswick Sports Hall of Fame. From the early 1900s until the mid-1920s, she dominated women's tennis in New Brunswick, winning fourteen provincial and three Maritime championships. As an early member of the Fredericton Golf Club, she continued to play long after she gave up tennis.

Golf became very popular. Women often took part in social events at clubs to which their husbands belonged, or they organized the popular luncheons and teas, but it was not until the early 1890s that they took up the game themselves. "Ladies" clubs (sections of existing clubs) began to appear, the first being at the Royal Montreal Golf Club in early 1892. Later that year, the

Violet (Pooley) Sweeny of Victoria, British Columbia, was an exceptional golfer between 1905 and 1930.

Royal Montreal Ladies' Golf Club held their first competition: thirteen women took part and the winner shot 150 over eighteen holes. In 1894, the Toronto Golf Club admitted women members, and within a year they numbered one hundred, almost half the club membership. Interclub matches began to flourish, especially in Toronto, where twenty or so golf clubs were in easy reach by train or tram (by 1900 there were about fifty golf clubs across the country).

The first official Dominion ladies' golf championship took place in Toronto in 1901, won by Lillias (Lilly) Young, star player at the Royal Montreal. Coming second was Mabel (Gordon) Thomson from Saint John, New Brunswick, whose strength was her long, raking wood shots. Essentially self-taught, she would go on to win the Canadian Ladies' Amateur Championship five times between 1902 and 1908, and represent

Canada in team matches in the United States and Britain during the same period.

Violet (Pooley) Sweeny of Victoria was another outstanding golfer of this era. She played in her first provincial championship in 1905, winning the title, and a month later won the Pacific Northwest championship. Over the next twenty-five years, Sweeny would capture eight more provincial titles and another six Pacific Northwest championships.

On the golf links, as everywhere else, women were expected to act in a modest and becoming manner. A Halifax pastor complained about women golfers swearing, although the editor of the Charlottetown *Morning Guardian* came to their defence, claiming that if they did swear, it was at "the imperfections and exasperations of men." What to wear was always a problem; most dressed in large hats, Norfolk jackets (often scarlet) worn over tailored shirts, and long skirts edged at the bottom with leather to protect them from wet grass. Many used a device called a "Miss Higgins," a band of elastic webbing slipped around their knees to keep their long skirts from blowing up and interfering with their shots. Slip-on golf shoes with little spikes went over the toes of regular shoes; knitted sweaters and golf capes became essential for cold, wet weather.

Golf was also the first sport in which Canadian women sought to control their own affairs. Florence Harvey, a member of the Hamilton Golf Club, won the Canadian Ladies' championship in 1903 and 1904 (beating out Mabel Thomson). In 1912, she went to England to play in the British championship, where she became acquainted with the work of the Ladies' Golf Union, especially in establishing a uniform system of handicapping, arranging annual championships, acting as a legislative body and promoting the game for women. It became apparent to Florence that Canadian women golfers needed a similar organization. She seized

Members of the Canadian Ladies' Golf Union in 1913; Florence Harvey is seated, centre.
Right: Mabel (Gordon) Thompson, from Saint John, New Brunswick, won the Canadian ladies' golf championship five times between 1902 and 1908.

the opportunity at a meeting on September 28, 1913, when two top British golfers came to play in the Canadian championship at the Royal Montreal Golf Club. They no doubt explained the benefits of the Ladies' Golf Union and promised their support to those in attendance. The Canadian Ladies' Golf Union (CLGU) was formed, with Frances Campbell of Toronto as president and Florence Harvey as organizing secretary. Likely the first women's sport executive in Canada, Florence proved to be an able administrator, quickly setting up three geographical divisions — Maritime (nine clubs), Middle (Quebec, Ontario and the Prairies with twenty-four clubs) and Pacific (four clubs) — further subdivided into districts, each with its own man-

ager. Ladies' sections of clubs who belonged to the CLGU paid annual dues of between ten and twenty dollars depending on their membership, with the money going towards the cost of administering the association and special medals purchased through the British organization.

Winter sports also attracted women of leisure and means. Although the Royal Montreal Curling Club dates from 1807, it was another eighty-seven years before women played there: the Ladies' Auxiliary Club was organized in 1894 through the efforts of a Mrs. E.A. Whitehead, who became its first president. This was probably the first women's curling Club in the world, since the stuffy Royal Caledonian Club in Scotland did not admit women until 1895, and even then did so

The first ladies' curling club in St. John's, Newfoundland, in 1906.

reluctantly. By 1900, the Montreal Ladies' Curling Club boasted about eighty ardent members and similar clubs had sprouted, mostly in Ontario and Quebec, whose towns were the first to build indoor rinks. Curling among women in western Canada had a slower start. Although two rinks of girls are reported to have played in Edmonton as early as 1893, it was not until 1908 that women in Winnipeg organized a club, and 1912 that women in Banff formed another; the first bonspiels took place in Edmonton and Winnipeg a couple of years later.

Skating was a thoroughly respectable pastime: "It is as natural for Quebec girls to skate," declared a national magazine, "as it is for other women to walk." Fancy skating was becoming popular — the Rideau Skating Club in Ottawa held a women's competition as early as 1890. Early governors general, and sometimes their wives and children, played a major role in promoting skating. Lord and Lady Minto (1898–1904) both excelled at the sport and hosted many lively skating parties during their time at Rideau Hall. The Minto Skating Club, which they founded in 1903, has produced many famous skaters. Lord Grey (1904–1911) founded the Earl Grey Skating Club in Montreal. The winner of the first Canadian Figure Skating Championship in 1905 was Anne Ewan from the Earl Grey Skating Club; she was followed by Aimee Haycock in 1906 and 1908 from the Minto Club in Ottawa. There was no competition in 1907 because the Minto Club burned down. Lord Grey's daughter Lady Evelyn Grey (Evelyn Jones) won the championship in 1911.

Young women roller skating in Sarnia, Ontario, in 1909.

In small towns, especially in southern Ontario, skating rinks were often the only existing sports facility, and at the same time a respectable space where both middle- and working-class single women could seek fun, exercise and male companionship. Although the cost of a season ticket ($2.50) was probably prohibitive for a working-class girl, ten or fifteen cents would allow entrance to a night's skating or sometimes a fancy carnival or masquerade. In the early to mid-1880s, commercial roller rinks began to appear in small towns, providing yet another popular and affordable space for young women to socialize and take some exercise.

"Whether sleighing, skating, snow-shoeing or tobogganing, young Canada's never happy without the fair sex," wrote an enthusiast in 1883, "and only on the long tramps of the snow-shoe clubs are ladies supposed to be absent." Ladies' nights became a feature of the snowshoe clubs, but they were allowed only on short tramps, with the remainder of the evening devoted to music, dancing and singing. The long tramps afforded an opportunity for male segregation and a particularly masochistic form of hibernal manliness: "on cross country tramps over hilly terrain under crisp, slippery snow conditions, snowshoes were broken, ankles were fractured, frostbite and blisters were common …." Speeches at annual club dinners of the Montreal Snowshoe Club repeatedly referred to the "moral bearing, independence and manliness" of snowshoers, whereas women "could only aspire to marry a snowshoe man."

Schools, colleges and universities allowed middle- and upper-class Victorian and Edwardian girls and young women the most freedom to explore their physicality and athleticism. The boring military drill, formal gymnastics and club swinging were slowly replaced by exciting sports like basketball and ice hockey. Basketball was the most popular sport for girls in high school, having been introduced around the turn of the century. It was likely their first chance to participate in an active sport requiring some physical exertion. In 1899, Nora Cleary, a teacher at the Windsor Collegiate Institute in

The McGill School of Physical Education basketball team in 1927, with coach Ethel Mary Cartwright third from the left in the back row.

Ontario, introduced the game to her students after she had sent for a basketball and rule book advertised in a booklet produced by the Spalding sporting goods company in the United States. The girls stood around while she read the rules and then they tried to play, soon becoming proficient enough to travel to Detroit to play other teams.

Colleges and universities began to hire specialist teachers in physical education to teach the growing numbers of women students. Ethel Mary Cartwright is a good example. She immigrated to Canada from England in 1904 when she was hired to teach physical culture to the young women of Halifax Ladies College. In 1906, she moved to Montreal to become Physical Director of Royal Victoria College at McGill University, a women-only institution financed by Lord Strathcona, who saw to it that a well-equipped gymnasium, available only to women, was built with the facility. Affectionately dubbed "Carty" by her students, she established a required physical education program for all first-year students, and by 1912 undergraduates needed to complete 140 hours of physical education before graduating. Her program consisted of dance, apparatus, free gymnastics, Indian-club swinging and sports instruction, especially in tennis and basketball.

Indian clubs were used, like dumbbells, for arm exercises as part of physical education programs in colleges and schools.

A strong supporter of competitive sport opportunities for her students, Carty helped them organize sports days, intramural events and, most important, intercollegiate competition with nearby universities.

Only a tiny fraction of the population attended a college or university, and among these, there were very few women. Increasing urbanization and industrialization at the turn of the century brought thousands of young, single "working girls" into the larger Canadian cities. They left the farms and small towns seeking work as seamstresses, milliners, office workers or store clerks, or as industrial workers in the expanding factories, or if need be, as domestic servants in private homes. By 1881, single women represented over 16 percent of Toronto's population, which ten years later had increased to 18.4 percent. By 1891, nearly two hundred factories in the city of Halifax employed over 1,200 women, most single and under twenty years old. Where daughters

from middle-class families, the so-called "New Women," took up comparatively well-paying jobs in commerce, education, government and the professions en route to marriage and a family, the vast majority of wage-earning working-class women worked because they had to.

The organization most interested in young, urbanized working girls was the Young Women's Christian Association (YWCA), which first began to sprout in major Canadian centres in the 1870s. By the mid-1880s, it strove to provide "legitimate amusements" to lure impressionable working girls away from the dance halls, movie theatres, saloons and pool halls, all of which were deemed unhealthy and suspect. By 1900, with fourteen branches established across the country, many in their own buildings with a cafeteria and gymnasium, sometimes a swimming pool, the YWCA had effectively become a women-centred athletic club. Between 1914 and 1915, for example, the number of registrants for

Top: Swimming lessons at the Toronto YWCA, conducted by instructor Mary Beaton in 1908.
Left: An early twentieth-century women's bathing suit with bloomers and a covering dress, typically made of wool serge or flannel.
Below: Images of women were used to attract male buyers to cigar brands. This one is from 1915.

"physical culture" had jumped from 766 to 3,558, largely because of the new pools or the possibility of using one of them in the nearby YMCA. The Toronto YWCA, one of the first to have a swimming pool, hired Mary Beaton, an accomplished Scottish swimmer and instructor, to conduct classes in swimming, water polo, lifesaving and fancy diving. After a session, the bulky wet bathing suits were hung up in a drying room and the swimmers dried their hair, bent over a long pipe extending from a small gas stove. By 1910, wrote one enthusiast, the YWCA had become the "axle round which all the physical culture of Toronto revolves."

In 1912, a young teacher named J. Percy Page moved from Ontario to Edmonton to help organize commercial courses in Edmonton high schools. Two years later he took charge of the commercial classes at the new McDougall High School, and with his assistant Ernest Hyde, organized boys' and girls' basketball teams even though the school had no gymnasium and home games had to be played outdoors. Hyde decided to coach the boys, leaving Page the girls. In the first year, Page guided his team to the high school championship with victories over the three other teams in the league; the next year they won the provincial championship. Since graduating players wanted to keep playing, they

Percy Page and students at McDougall High School, Edmonton, 1917.

formed the Commercial Athletic Society with the purpose of forming a team after they graduated. By 1917 they were known as the Edmonton Commercial Graduates (the "Grads" for short), and over the next two decades, mostly because of their phenomenal success, they were to have a remarkable effect on the growth of women's basketball in Canada.

Another team sport with an early history of community participation among Canadian girls and women is ice hockey; the first teams appeared in the early 1890s. Just who was the first is uncertain, but one of the earliest written accounts was of a game between two teams, simply designated as numbers one and two, in Ottawa on February 11, 1891. Photographs of women's hockey teams dating from this period support the claim that teams existed, if only for social reasons and before the development of leagues and competitions. Early women's ice hockey in Quebec, for example, was very much a social affair, with mostly English-speaking young women of *la meilleure société* participating. At the turn of the century, clubs existed in Montreal (anglophone Westmount), Trois Rivières, Lachute and Quebec City. Matches were often played for charity, or a special occasion, such as a send-off for Canadian soldiers going to the Boer War. At the first

Women playing ice hockey in Toronto circa 1910.

women's hockey game ever played in Montreal, by members of the newly formed Quebec Ladies' Hockey Club, $125 was raised for the Soldiers' Wives League. The reporting of women's hockey in newspapers of this era was rare because games were played informally and infrequently. In 1902, a challenge match organized between the Ladies' Hockey clubs of Trois-Rivières and Montreal was considered the championship of Canada since there were no organized leagues and tournaments, and certainly no opportunity to travel very far.

By the early 1900s and certainly by the First World War, women's hockey teams were organized in communities small and large throughout Canada, from the Maritimes to British Columbia and as far north as the Yukon. They played mostly outdoors because indoor arenas were rare. They also played mostly among themselves, although leagues made up of teams from neighbouring towns and cities began to be organized. In 1906, for example, the first Alberta provincial tournament was held at the Banff Winter Carnival with six teams competing, and in 1914 Ontario women competed in Picton at their first provincial championship.

Although major tournaments were cancelled during the war, and Dominion and provincial championships postponed, women often competed in local and club tournaments in order to raise funds for the Red Cross, prisoners of war or the war effort in general. Within the private sports clubs their participation increased, often to support patriotic causes, and because men were at war they took on more organizational responsibility, which would reap benefits for them when the war ended.

Chapter Three

GIRLS' SPORT RUN BY GIRLS

On May 12, 1922, The Edmonton Commercial Graduates basketball team left Edmonton to make the long train journey east to play the London Shamrocks for the first Dominion women's championship. Before 1,500 spectators, the Grads beat the Shamrocks 41–8 in the first game, played under the six-player "girls' rules" to the advantage of the western team. The Grads went down to defeat 21–8 in the second game, mainly because the five-player "boys' rules" were used to the Shamrocks' benefit. When the Grads returned ten days later, having won the title on overall points, a large and boisterous crowd, including the mayor, city councillors, school board officials and several hundred students, was at the train station to welcome them. Every newspaper in the country carried the story of these six young women, now Canadian champions — Dorothy and Daisy Johnson, Winnie Martin, Eleanor Mountifield, Nellie Perry and Connie Smith — all graduates of McDougall High School, and their former teacher, Percy Page, who had coached them to victory.

Smartly turned out in black and gold middies with knee-length bloomers, heavy woollen socks, pads to protect their knees, and hair-bands to keep long locks out of their eyes, the Grads were fit, athletic and feminine, fast and skilled on the court, and the very model of womanhood off it. A columnist at the *Toronto Star* repeatedly assured his readers the athletes were women, still "essentially feminine" and "lithe, bounding, immeasurably light on their small feet." He tried

to avoid condescension, although not always successfully, writing that his intent was to give the girls a boost: "For the fact of the matter is,

The Underwood Trophy, presented annually (from 1926 to 1963) to the winners of the Canadian Women's Basketball Championship.

1922 Edmonton Grads: left to right are Daisy Johnson, coach Percy Page, Nellie Perry, Eleanor Mountifield, Dorothy Johnson, Winnie Martin and Connie Smith.

unquestionably, that the girls are athletes of the very first rank, that their comprehension of the sport is quite as complete as any male team of any description, and the grace with which they do it is utterly and forever beyond the power of males." Under "Papa Page," the Grads trained and practised hard, sometimes with boys' teams, but, away from the basketball floor, they were expected to dress and behave like the reputable young working women they were. They helped fashion a new model of athletic womanhood, characterized by the masculine qualities of skill,

strength, speed, agility and energy, while at the same time retaining their femininity. Their very presence helped redefine the earlier contested notions of womanhood.

Often referred to as the golden age of women's sports, the 1920s was a time when women began experimenting and competing seriously in new sports, at the same time consolidating their hold on others. Nothing seemed to hold them back. There was a growing public enchantment with these new stars of the athletic world and the sports press obliged by reporting their exploits and, for the most part, treating them seriously. "Canadian women are not just knocking at the door of the world of sport," observed a male sportswriter; "they have crashed the gate, swarmed the field and, in some cases, have driven mere man to the sidelines."

The first woman to represent Canada at an Olympic Games was Cecil Eustace Smith. In 1924, at the first official Winter Games in Chamonix, France, Smith competed in the ladies' figure skating competition, the only event for women on the limited program. Cecil and her older sister Maude were introduced to skating on the frozen ponds and backyards of their neighbourhood close to the Toronto Skating Club. They belonged to an adventuresome and outgoing family, attended a private school where sports were stressed, and were supported by their mother, the former Maude Delano-Osborne, who in 1892 had won the first Canadian ladies' tennis championship.

In 1922, Cecil was the junior ladies champion, and the following year was runner-up in the Canadian championship, beaten only by Dorothy Jenkins of the Minto Club in Ottawa. She teamed up with Melville Rogers, the men's champion, and the two were chosen to represent Canada in an official world's skating championship — the 1924 Olympics in France. Only fifteen, Cecil was accompanied by her mother and sister, along with the rest of the fifteen-member Canadian Olympic team comprising her pairs partner Rogers, the lone speed skater Charlie Gorman, and the Granites, a hockey team.

Much to her surprise, Cecil was a hit with the British and European press, who singled out the only Canadian female competitor for her beauty and lively personality. On the day of the competition, the temperature dropped considerably, making conditions on the outdoor ice rink troublesome, and to top it off, Cecil was not called in time, and she had to rush over to the

Cecil Eustace Smith, the first woman to represent Canada at an Olympic Games.

bitterly cold rink "benumbed and breakfastless" to perform her compulsory figures. She did better in the free skate, but in the end came sixth, two places ahead of eleven-year-old Sonja Henie, the Norwegian sensation who was to dominate women's skating for the next two decades. Smith and Rogers were seventh in the pairs competition, although everyone expected them to place much higher, bringing about accusations in Canadian news reports that politics influenced the judging (some things never change).

Ada MacKenzie, Canada's most outstanding woman golfer throughout the 1920s and 1930s, years later at the club she founded, with junior golfer Sandra Post.

Cecil went on to win the Canadian ladies championship in 1925 and 1926, and at the Olympics in St. Moritz in 1928 came fifth (Sonja Henie won the gold). A few years later in 1930, she became the first Canadian to win a world skating championship medal, when she came second (again behind Sonja Henie) at Madison Square Garden in New York City.

Maude and Cecil Smith, and especially Cecil, became fine golfers. As members of the Toronto Golf Club, they were coached by professional George Cumming, joining the many known as "Cumming girls" because of their distinctive swing. If women wanted to play golf, they had to play in clubs controlled by men and under the rules they established. Many women who played were business or professional women, those who worked at jobs during the day, and yet Saturdays and Sundays at the clubs were often reserved for men. Ada MacKenzie, Canada's outstanding female golfer of this era, decided to do something about this. She took out an option on some land in Thornhill, Toronto, raised capital through a bond issue, sold $100 memberships to three hundred women, and supervised the construction of the clubhouse and course. The Toronto Ladies' Golf Club opened in 1924, and today remains one of the premier clubs in North America — and still open only to women.

Working-class women who flocked to the cities before and during the war seeking employment in the factories, stores and businesses had little hope of attending college or university, where women's sport was well established and flourishing. Nor could they afford to belong to the elite tennis, golf and curling clubs. They sought instead to expand their sporting opportunities and athletic presence through a grassroots movement that established women's athletic clubs, organizations and leagues in an increasing variety of sports, although the staples were basketball, ice hockey, softball and athletics.

Individual sponsors, businesses, factories, municipalities and sometimes women themselves provided the necessary equipment, uniforms and facilities to allow them to play and compete. Organizational support and leadership came from existing men's sports clubs, church and youth organizations, large and small businesses, sports entrepreneurs and, increasingly, from women sports leaders determined to administer their own sports.

The Toronto Ladies Athletic Club, for example, was founded in 1921 by a group of women athletes, among them Alexandrine Gibb, who became its first president. After completing school, Alex worked as a secretary, but in her spare time was an aspiring sportswriter and an enthusiastic organizer, administrator and promoter of women's sport. Her philosophy, "girls' sport run by girls," was uncompromising, and put into practice through the Toronto Ladies Athletic Club, an exclusively women's organization with teams in several sports (basketball, softball, track and field) all coached and managed by women.

Alex Gibb also founded the more ambitious Canadian Ladies Athletic Club to provide sporting opportunities for girls and women across the country but it never caught on except in Toronto and Montreal. More successful, and also her brainchild, was the Women's Amateur Athletic Federation of Canada, which eventually established branches across the country and, until 1954, controlled women's sport (mainly athletics) when it amalgamated with the men's organization.

Fanny "Bobbie" Rosenfeld, Myrtle Cook, Grace Conacher and Rosa Grosse at the 1923 CNE.

These newly formed sports clubs were the most active promoters of women's track and field; they provided facilities, coaches, practice time, competitions and, most significant of all, the notion that keeping records about who could run the fastest, jump the highest or throw the farthest was important, certainly if Canadian girls were going to test themselves against the rest of the world.

In September 1923, the Canadian National Exhibition in Toronto sponsored a 100-yard dash and a relay race for women. Four sprinters and their coach, the "Chicago Flyers," were invited to provide an international flavour. Ninety girls entered, and among them were Fanny ("Bobbie") Rosenfeld, Myrtle Cook, Grace Conacher, Rosa Grosse — Canadian athletes who were well known but mostly in other sports. While the Chicago quartet was attired in eye-fetching shorts and clinging jerseys, the

Canadians were a motley crew in blue serge bloomers with blousy middies. Bobbie looked even more comical in her brother's swimming trunks and the white top of her Hinde and Dauch softball uniform. Much to the astonishment of 15,000 spectators, Bobbie and Rosa came first and second in the 100-yard final, beating the United States champion, and the Canadians, who had never competed together before, came first in the relay.

Across the country, women with a talent for running began training seriously even though there was little chance of their competing internationally. Since the men who controlled sport were vehemently opposed to including women's track and field events in the Summer Olympics, women decided to take matters into their own hands. In 1922, French sportswoman Alice Milliat, and her newly formed Fédération sportive féminine internationale (FSFI), organized a spectacular international track and field event in Paris and called it the Jeux olympiques

The 1928 Canadian women's Olympic team before departing for Amsterdam: (front row from the left) Ethel Smith, Jean Thompson, Myrtle Cook, Dorothy Prior, Jane Bell and Bobbie Rosenfeld. Peeking through in the back row are chaperone Marie Parkes, manager Alexandrine Gibb, and Ethel Catherwood.

féminins. Canadian women (led by Alex Gibb) were now motivated to organize track and field through provincial championships so they could find the best competitors. The battle between the FSFI and the International Amateur Athletic Federation over who would control women's athletics came to a truce of sorts when the IAAF offered to include several track events (as an experiment) on the 1928 Olympic program. There would be five events in total: 100-metre, 800-metre, high jump, 4x100-metre relay, and discus. Canadian athletes now had something to set their sights on.

The 1928 Canadian track and field championships and Olympic trials were held in Halifax. Six women athletes were selected to represent Canada: Ethel Smith, Myrtle Cook, Bobbie Rosenfeld, Florence (Jane) Bell, Ethel Catherwood and Jean Thompson. Among them were high school students, office secretaries, a factory worker and a business college student. They trained either at the Toronto Ladies or the Parkdale Ladies'

Myrtle Cook, at left, winning a preliminary heat in the 100-metre at the 1928 Olympics.
Bottom: Myrtle Cook's leather running shoes with spikes.

Athletic Club also in Toronto. Ethel Catherwood, the "Saskatoon lily," had been enticed to Parkdale by the flamboyant Fred G. "Teddy" Oke, a former hockey player, war veteran and self-made millionaire, whose largesse sponsored women athletes and teams.

Canada's six track entries at the 1928 Olympics in Amsterdam were joined by sixteen-year-old swimmer Dorothy Prior of the Parkdale-Dolphinet Club in Toronto, with her expenses paid by Teddy Oke. The story of the

Ethel Catherwood clears the bar at 5'2" to win the women's high jump at the 1928 Olympics.

amazing "Matchless Six" has been told and retold: a gold and world record in the high jump by Ethel Catherwood; also gold and world record for the Cook-Rosenfeld-Smith-Bell relay team; a silver and bronze for Rosenfeld and Smith in the 100-metre; and a fourth and fifth for Rosenberg and Thompson in the 800-metre. The small Canadian contingent won more points than any other nation. They came home to an ecstatic welcome, both in Montreal and in Toronto, and were showered with gifts including diamond-studded wristwatches given to them by the Canadian National Exhibition.

Fanny ("Bobbie" because she bobbed her hair) Rosenfeld was the most famous and admired Canadian woman athlete in this era. This Russian-born daughter of Jewish immigrants was raised in Barrie, Ontario, but while still in high school moved with her family to Toronto, where she found work as a stenographer at the

Patterson Chocolate factory. Obviously a fine runner, she also excelled at hockey, basketball and softball. She could do it all. Sadly, her athletic career was prematurely cut short by arthritis so she turned to coaching and managing, and most importantly, to sports writing. She started out at the *Montreal Herald* before settling in at the *Globe and Mail*, where her column, "Feminine Sports Reel," appeared from 1937 to 1958.

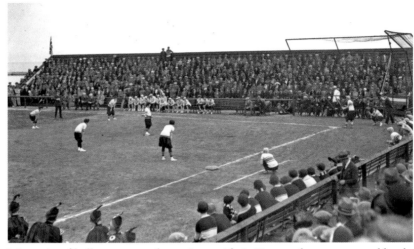

Women's softball was so popular at Sunnyside in Toronto that permanent bleachers were erected for the opening game of the 1925 season.

Bobbie was one of several well-known athletes who became sportswriters. The first was Alexandrine Gibb, who in 1928 began writing her "No Man's Land of Sport" column on a regular basis for the *Toronto Daily Star*; it continued until 1940. Phyllis Griffiths, a keen basketball player, landed her first job at the *Toronto Telegram* and by 1928 had her own sports column, "The Girl and the Game," a fixture until 1942. Myrtle Cook began her career as a sportswriter with the *Montreal Star* in 1929, writing her column "In the Women's Sportlight" for over forty years. Similar columns began to sprout up all over the country in daily newspapers. It was not unusual in those days for sports reporters to be actively engaged in the organizations they covered. Not only did these early women sportswriters chronicle the development of women's sport in Canada between the wars, but they also helped to create it.

Team sports, especially basketball, ice hockey and softball, flourished across the country as more and more cities, towns and smaller communities sponsored teams and leagues. Most leagues were localized, or at best provincial, because travel across the country was arduous and expensive. Basketball was also hindered by the "rules" problem. Teams in the east played mostly the restrictive, six-player, no-dribbling "girls' rules," whereas western teams used the five-player, full-court "boys' rules" (the Grads switched in 1922 to these rules). When east met west, it sometimes required the use of both sets of rules in the same match, with girls' rules being played one game, boys' the next, and both used in a final game if necessary.

Ice hockey was no longer a game played primarily by women in universities or from the more bourgeois sectors of society, because thousands of working-class girls took up the sport with enormous enthusiasm. It had a wide following among factory workers, department store clerks, secretaries and the like, especially in small towns, and slowly they began to organize themselves into leagues and organizations. The Ladies Ontario Hockey Association appears to be among the first, when twenty senior clubs from

An early women's speed skating contest with Lela Brooks (far left) in the lead.
Below: A battered pair of speed skates, worn by Lela Brooks.

all parts of Ontario were represented at an inaugural meeting in December 1922.

Women's softball exploded across the country. At Toronto's Sunnyside, for example, teams were attracting huge crowds of up to 9,000 for regularly scheduled games several nights each week. On the prairies, and particularly in Saskatchewan, it spread like wildfire. There was already a tradition of women's baseball in the larger centres, but many switched to softball because it was easier to play, required less formal settings and they had been introduced to the sport in school or on the playground.

Speed skating attracted increasing numbers of women. Two skaters who received a great deal of press attention in this era were Gladys Robinson and Lela Brooks. Gladys learned to skate at a young age, having grown up near the Aura Lee rink in Toronto, and by the age of fourteen she was the Canadian women's speed skating champion. Her coach was Fred Robson, who before the war and at the peak of his career had held nine world records. In 1920, when she was eighteen, Robinson competed in the world speed skating championship at Lake Placid, New York, the first time the International Skating Union allowed women to compete, and in a field of eighteen she came third. It was unusual for a promising woman athlete to have a personal coach in those days, but Robson devised a program of skating, walking, running, skipping and strength-building exercises for his young athlete, trimming off a few pounds in the process. Their hard work paid off and in the following year, again at Lake Placid, she won all her events. Gladys went on to further success, often breaking a world record when she raced, and retired undefeated when she got married. Tragically, she died in 1934 at age thirty-two following a lengthy illness.

Start of the women's marathon swimming race at the CNE in 1928, where grease-coated swimmers removed their swim suits once they were in the water.

Described as an "entirely unaffected, supremely modest, completely normal Canadian schoolgirl," who skates like a "lightning demon," sixteen-year-old Lela Brooks from the Old Orchard Skating Club in Toronto established herself as a world-class speed skater in 1925 when she won the Canadian championships in three distances as well as major competitions in various cities throughout the United States. In 1926, she broke six world records and won the world championships, which were held in Saint John, New Brunswick. She came to the attention of sports promoter Teddy Oke, who sponsored her early competitive forays into the United States. She married early at eighteen, but continued to compete under the name Lela Brooks Potter well into the 1930s.

Marathon swimming was one of the first sports in which women could make money, sometimes big money although the earliest events do not mention money or prizes of any sort. On the west coast, an early woman competitor was Audrey Griffin, who began racing in 1915 when still a teenager. She swam (and usually won) every distance from fifty yards to three

Audrey Griffin of Vancouver usually won the annual "Through-Victoria Swim," a gruelling, cold, three-mile race.

miles, but her main claim to fame was winning the annual "Through-Victoria Swim" nine times in the twelve races she entered between 1915 and 1929. Although only three miles, it was a gruelling, cold swim from the old causeway float in front of the Empress Hotel up the waterway to the Gorge Bridge, with up to 10,000 spectators lining the course.

The most lucrative prizes in marathon swimming for both men and women were in Toronto at the Canadian National Exhibition. The first CNE/Wrigley (sponsored by chewing-gum magnate William Wrigley) marathon swim was held at the end of August in 1927. It was an open event over a twenty-one-mile course (actually a seven-mile triangle completed three times) with $50,000 in prize money ($8,000 for women alone) — a huge amount of money in those days. The event attracted nearly two hundred swimmers, but very few were women. Only three brave souls survived the frigid waters to complete the race, none of them female, although prize money was awarded to the four women who swam the furthest, one being a young Toronto swimmer, Edith Hedin.

The CNE marathon races continued in 1928 but this time there was a separate 10-mile event for women, with a prize offering of $15,000. The more lucrative ($35,000) men's event was held on another day, but it was also open to the top five women finishers, which seemed eminently fair. The rules mandated that once they were in the water swimmers could remove their swimsuits to be picked up by a following boat. Bathing suits in those days were often made of wool, a real drag in the water, and most swimmers coated themselves with axle grease to protect them from the cold. Putting all modesty aside, women too must have done this because it explains the photos of competitors at the start and finish of the race with bare chests. Canadian women rarely won the CNE marathon swims, although they sometimes placed in the prize money.

The 1920s had brought significant change to Canadian women's sport with the growth of teams and leagues, especially those sponsored by industrial concerns, the beginning of international competition primarily in track and field, and the increasing control by women over the administrative affairs of their sports. Although not everyone was wholeheartedly in favour of these developments, the 1930s would bring about unprecedented participation among Canadian sportswomen.

Chapter Four

PUSHING THE BOUNDARIES

Andy Lytle, sports editor at the *Vancouver Sun*, sparked a debate in 1933 when he called women athletes "leathery-limbed, flat-chested girls." Alex Gibb and other women sportswriters mounted a spirited defence of female athleticism in their columns and articles. In a rebuttal article published in *Chatelaine*, Bobbie Rosenfeld argued that women athletes were "paragons of feminine physique, beauty and health," and not the "Amazons and ugly ducklings" depicted by Lytle. She sneered at his claim that certain sports (ice hockey for one) were injurious to the health and physical development of women — "plain, ordinary, everyday tommyrot" — although she agreed that boxing and wrestling were "shouldn'ts."

In a much discussed article in *Maclean's*, Elmer Ferguson, sports editor of the *Montreal Star*, wrote that he was disgusted by the "violent, face-straining, face-dirtying, body-bouncing, sweaty, graceless, stumbling, struggling, wrenching, racking, jarring, and floundering" athletic events in which some girls engaged. He preferred women athletes with "grace, sweetness, rhythm, freedom from sweat and freedom from grime," accomplished only by speed and figure skaters, high divers, swimmers and many golf and tennis players. All the more "robust" forms of athletics, including "sprinting, jumping, hurdling, heaving weights, sliding into bases, struggling weakly and gracelessly around armed with hockey sticks or crashing each other at basketball in a sweat-reeking gymnasium," according to Ferguson, did nothing to enhance their femininity, and certainly not their sex appeal.

Alexandrine Gibb was an athlete, pioneering leader and administrator of women's sport, and Canada's pre-eminent woman sports journalist in the 1920s and 1930s.

Roxy Aitkins, an Olympic hurdler and women's sport organizer, penned a lively, well-argued defence in a subsequent issue. She astutely pointed out that most girls and women could not afford the costs of figure skating, golf or tennis, and that swimming and diving were also out for those in small communities with no access to pools, whereas available to both rich and poor, urban and rural were countless tracks,

Ruth Wilson was an all-round athlete who wrote a women's sports column for the Vancouver Sun *in the 1940s.*

softball diamonds, hockey rinks and gymnasiums. It was through sports like basketball, track, softball and hockey, she argued, that "many young girls, who were thin, scrawny, unattractive, prone to mixing with boy gangs, and pointed for trouble ahead" were physically developed through exercise and fresh air, disciplined by training, broadened by travel, and socially enriched through contact with older girls and chaperones. Her final plea: "Girls are human beings. They want an equal chance with men to go places, to see the world, to parade before the crowds, to win medals and cups, to hear the cheers of spectators. They want a chance to play, to develop physically, to cultivate the spirit of sportsmanship, to meet nice people, to have an interest beyond the home and office."

Echoing earlier criticisms, a concern raised frequently in the popular press was whether "stressful and intense" athletic competition would harm women's reproductive capacity. Sportswriter Frederick Griffin, in an article published in the *Toronto Star Weekly*, was typical of those asking questions about whether sports were making girls "tough under the skin" or "hurting them physically." What he was really asking was whether they would make good wives and mothers by being able to reproduce the "race." He surveyed a variety of experts, including a well-known gynaecologist in Toronto who agreed that fit women make healthier mothers, but patronizingly suggested that women athletes made better child bearers because they obeyed doctors during pregnancy and labour, just as they would a coach. Griffin also gathered statistics from Percy Page about former Edmonton Grads who had married and had babies (only one married ex-Grad was so far childless).

Alex Gibb pointed out that "star" athletes were not neglecting motherhood and provided a list of recent examples including Olympic medal winner and sportswriter Myrtle Cook McGowan and sprinter Rosa Grosse O'Neill, both retired from the track, as well as others less well known. Women sports columnists kept careful track of the marital status and reproductive capacity of former well-known athletes by announcing engagements, marriages and births and, if they didn't have anything concrete to announce along marital lines, hinted at an imminent "sport romance."

Not only were women sportswriters pitted against their male counterparts, they also were forced to counter the arguments (and actions) of women physical educators opposed to high-level sport for girls and women. Many physical educators promoted "play for play's sake," stressing the enjoyment of sport and the development of good sportsmanship and character, rather than the breaking of records and the winning of championships. Although in their view athletic competition for girls and women was thoroughly desirable and beneficial, totally unacceptable were intense and highly specialized contests such as interschool and intercollegiate sport, and certainly the Olympics.

Their philosophy was encapsulated in the creed "a team for every girl and every girl on the team," best accomplished through a broadly based intramural sports program that exposed students to a variety of athletic experiences. Also popular were "play days," where girls from different institutions, whether elementary or high schools, colleges or universities, industrial, civic or church groups, met for a day of games and athletics. Play days, they argued, would effectively eliminate spectators, publicity, gate receipts and individual stars, indeed all forms of commercialization and exploitation. To remove all traces of the "evils" of men's sport, they advocated a separatist philosophy whereby only women administered, coached, officiated, and controlled girls' and women's sports.

It was in this context that women physical educators in Toronto, and a few other areas in Ontario, withdrew their schools from interschool competition in the early 1930s. The policy was divisive since the majority of schools continued to compete, and some even added new sports. In her sports column, Bobbie Rosenfeld complained bitterly about the cancellation, relying on the old adage that only athletic competition teaches the true meaning of sportsmanship.

Women sportswriters were hitting at the heart of differences between the middle-class, university-educated, professional physical educators, and the promoters of popular sports (many of whom were men) for the thousands of young Canadian working women now enjoying increasing opportunities to play, recreate and compete. Alex Gibb's position was that commercial or industrial sport was the only opportunity for the thousands of young women who worked in the factories, shops and downtown businesses to play sport at all. "The girls lure the commercial

Noel MacDonald was the star centre for the Edmonton Grads basketball team from 1933 to 1939.

The Caledonia Indians, with players drawn mostly from the Six Nations Reserve in Ontario, were a highly successful softball team in the 1930s.

firms into supporting them, so they can play ball under proper circumstances, be properly clad with clothing and have bats and balls and fun."

And play they did. Debates over strenuous competition or innuendoes about "mannish" athletes were of little concern to the thousands of girls and young women now participating in unprecedented numbers in softball, basketball, hockey, track and field, swimming and a host of new sports like bowling, badminton, alpine skiing, competitive cycling, even cricket. Development did not take place evenly across the country; some sports struggled in some regions, but thrived in others.

On the prairies, during the terrible drought-laden years of the Depression, many considered softball a "godsend." Ball diamonds were everywhere, the game was cheap to play and required a minimum of equipment, and it was fun and exciting, providing a much-needed distraction. Just about every rural Saskatchewan community had a "ladies" softball team, who travelled by horseback, foot or truck to practise on a rough

diamond laid out in a nearby farmer's field.

Softball was also popular among Aboriginal women, especially those who lived on reserves. The "Caledonia Indians," for instance, came mostly from the Six Nations Reserve along the Grand River in Ontario. The team had both white and Aboriginal women, and off the reserve they played exhibition games in southern Ontario including the leagues in Toronto. Sportswriter Phyllis Griffith once announced: "INDIANS ARE COMING … The Indians have several honest-to-goodness Indians in their lineup, and are a good team into the bargain." A racist remark by today's standards, but it points to how unusual it was for Aboriginal women to be seen playing competitive sport in the 1930s.

Softball was a tough game, and players frequently got hurt. Women sports columnists dutifully reported the various league injuries from minor cuts, bruises and dislocations, to seriously broken bones and concussions. Injured players were assisted through a league's emergency fund, and exhibition games were held periodically to raise money for this purpose. Until well into the 1930s, at Sunnyside in Toronto, only the catcher and player on first base could use mitts, and shoes with spikes were never allowed. Players wore long socks with no skin showing between their shorts and legs, although teams from the United States kept their socks rolled down, prompting Alex Gibb to joke that if the Canadians wanted to attract more spectators, they too should bare their legs. International contests with teams like the

Cleveland Erin Brews, Chicago Down Drafts and Detroit Rainbows played to capacity crowds of 3,000 crammed into Sunnyside — no comparison, however, to the 14,000 fans who in the spring of 1939 watched Langley's Lakesides (managed by Bobbie Rosenfeld) play exhibition softball at Madison Square Garden in New York.

While softball flourished, ice hockey struggled to maintain its earlier dominance. Organized and played unevenly across the country, the game was strong in the Maritimes, in decline throughout Quebec, disorganized in Ontario except for the north where it thrived, and in the west was robust, mostly in Alberta.

The Preston Rivulettes dominated Canadian women's ice hockey in the 1930s.

Ontario's Preston Rivulettes dominated Canadian women's hockey in the 1930s by winning 350 games, tying 3, and losing only 2. Their only defeat came in 1933 when they travelled to Edmonton to challenge the Western Canadian champions, the Edmonton Rustlers, for the first Dominion title, and lost in two games. After that, they won the Ontario title every year, and the Canadian championship (in the years it was played), until the team disbanded in 1941. Without balanced competition, interest in hockey waned; the cost of equipment and lack of ice time posed insurmountable problems for some teams, and many completely disappeared.

Canadian women's basketball in the 1930s was dominated by the unbeatable Edmonton Grads, still coached by Percy Page, who worked incessantly to promote his team and find them suitable competition. Although the Grads played

a major role in establishing and promoting women's basketball nationally, even internationally, their supremacy over all contenders became a hindrance to developing worthy opponents across the country.

A serious problem in promoting women's basketball across the country was the contentious issue of differing rules. A 1941 survey showed there was still an even east-west split, with British Columbia, Alberta, Saskatchewan and Manitoba governed almost entirely by men's rules, whereas Ontario, Quebec, New Brunswick and Nova Scotia accounted for most of the 53 percent using girls' rules. A handful of women physical education teachers in private schools, a few high schools and YWCAs tried to introduce the girls' game in the western provinces but with limited success. Similarly, there were organized leagues using men's rules in eastern Canada, but

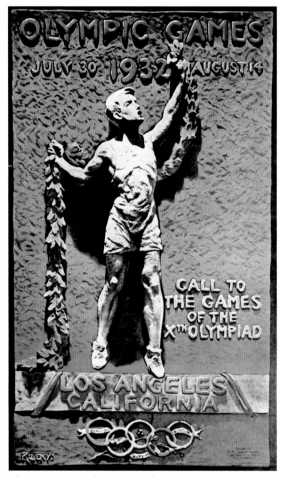

The 1932 Canadian women's Summer Olympic team was the largest yet sent into international competition.

they were almost entirely outside the schools, universities and teacher training colleges.

On the international stage, Canadian women athletes continued to show they were among the best. The 1932 women's Summer Olympic team was the largest yet sent into international competition, with nine track athletes, nine swimmers and divers, and one lone fencer, a major accomplishment in the midst of the Depression. Canada came away with a silver medal in the women's 100-metre, when "tiny" Hilda Strike, coached by Myrtle Cook McGowan, was edged out at the tape by Stanislawa Walasiewicz (Stella Walsh) of Poland. Strike also anchored the women's 4x100-metre relay team (with Mildred Fizzell, Lillian Palmer and Mary Frizzel), only to be just beaten again at the tape by the United States, who won the gold. Eva Dawes, Canada's outstanding high jumper, won the bronze medal behind Americans Jean Shiley and the yet-to-be-famous Mildred "Babe" Didrikson.

Jean Wilson of Toronto was the outstanding performer in women's speed skating, a demonstration sport at the 1932 Winter Olympics in Lake Placid, New York, winning a gold and a silver and narrowly missing another first because she fell before the finish line. Still exceptional was the reigning queen of speed skating Lela Brooks Potter, who in her 1000- and 1500-metre heats broke the world records. Tragically, Jean Wilson fell ill not long after returning from Lake Placid, and died at age twenty-three of a degenerative muscle disease.

The second British Empire Games, held in London, England, in August of 1934, produced Canada's first outstanding female swimmer in international competition. She was nineteen-year-old Phyllis Dewar from Moose Jaw, Saskatchewan, who broke three records, and returned home with four gold medals. Called a "queen of swimmers, the greatest naiad that Canada has ever produced," she was gloriously feted upon returning home.

The German-organized 1936 Winter Olympics in Garmish-Partenkirchen showed how little support Canadian athletes received in this era, especially in international competition, due to the Depression and government apathy. The Canadian team had no uniforms so they bought their own white jackets and sewed on maple leaves. For the first time in the Winter Olympics, women skiers competed in a combined downhill-slalom event. Canada's entries, among them Diana Gordon Lennox, who distinguished herself by wearing a monocle, were living in England or Europe at the time, and after a brief training session in Grindlewald, Switzerland, before the Olympics, they went off to Germany at their own expense. They were not very successful.

Despite uneasiness over Hitler's rise to power in Nazi Germany and increasing evidence of atrocities against Jews, there was little support in Canada for a boycott of the 1936 Olympics in Berlin. Canada's high-jumper on the 1936 women's team was Margaret Bell, a member of the Vancouver Athletic Club. She was one of the few track and field athletes to make the team from outside the Toronto area — there were difficulties in getting athletes to the Dominion trials in Montreal, held just before the team departed in mid-July. The cost of sending each athlete to Berlin was about $300, a great deal of money in those days, and it was not unusual that some athletes were added to the team if they were able to raise the necessary travel funds, which made the selection process suspect. The track athletes did not do particularly well in Berlin, coming eighth overall, and Margaret Bell came a disappointing ninth in her event. Although there was no women's basketball in the Olympics, the Edmonton Grads were also in Berlin, having just completed a nine-game, undefeated European tour, in which they outscored their opponents 697 to 105.

The last major international competition of the 1930s, and, as it turned out, until after the Second World War, was the British Empire Games in February 1938 held in Sydney, Australia, a very long way by boat. Canadian athletes had to find their own way to Vancouver, the point of departure, and be prepared to be away nearly three months. Notable on the team was a young Vancouver sprinter, Barbara Howard, in all likelihood the first woman of colour to com-

Sprinter Barbara Howard (left), the first Canadian woman of colour to compete internationally, and high jumper Margaret Bell, both from Vancouver.

pete on an international team for Canada. Only seventeen and still in high school, Howard was as surprised as the team selectors when she outran several well-known sprinters at the western time trials; in fact, she equalled the British Empire Games record of 11.2 seconds. She was touted as a potential medal winner, but ended up sixth in the final of the 100-yard sprint.

On November 26, 1940, *Toronto Star* sportswriter Alex Gibb wrote in her women's sport column: "So long until the summertime. Keep your chin up but not out. I'll be seeing you. C'est la guerre! C'est la vie and au revoir to sports!" She was given responsibility for editing the *Star*'s

Hilda Strike was a star Canadian athlete at the 1932 Summer Olympics.

section on women's war work in Toronto, mostly about their efforts to raise money, sew and mend uniforms, and operate canteens and "hostess houses" for the troops. Alex never returned to her daily sports column (she died in 1958). Other women's sports columns disappeared too.

The war brought changes for women's sport, some bad and some good. Facilities were taken over by the forces, making practices and competitions difficult, especially indoor track and field, which relied on existing armouries. By 1940, the Edmonton Arena, home to the Edmonton Grads, had been taken over by the RCAF, forcing the Grads to practise and play elsewhere — that summer they disbanded. The war also brought annoying equipment shortages: "Give softball

bats loving care because they're as hard to get as a waiter's eye," advised Bobbie Rosenfeld.

Male coaches disappeared as more and more young men joined the forces and went overseas, with women taking over the coaching and training, and whatever else they had to do to keep their sports going. Well-known women athletes and officials joined the many voluntary service corps, or were recruited into the armed forces, and became too busy to continue with sport. Competitions, especially Dominion tournaments, were routinely cancelled, as were all European and world championships, including the 1940 and 1944 Olympics.

Although many women entered the armed forces during the war, and thousands more laboured in the war industries, the vast majority of Canadian women contributed to the war effort through unpaid labour in the home or volunteer work in their community, and sportswomen were no exception. Across the country there were countless examples of local women's sport groups raising money for a variety of war-related projects and agencies. The Canadian Ladies Golf Union, for instance, postponed all national and provincial championships and used golf as a means to raise money for war charities such as the Red Cross. Through tournaments, individual club donations, and by selling a poster with the word "Spitfire" in golf tees, the CLGU sent $40,000 to the Wings for Britain Fund. In all, the CLGU raised more than $81,000 during the war years, enough for two aeroplanes, and CLGU sewing rooms turned out thousands of clothes for war-stricken victims.

Like millions of ordinary Canadians, women athletes and sport organizations contributed to the overall war effort. Although sport suffered, it recovered quickly in the immediate postwar era, but with a different emphasis and perspective. Like all areas of social life in postwar Canada, change was inevitable.

Chapter Five

SWEETHEART HEROINES

At the 1947 World Figure Skating championships in Stockholm, eighteen-year-old Barbara Ann Scott was first in the compulsory school figures that were skated in freezing conditions on an outdoor rink. Before 15,000 cheering spectators in the free-skating competition, she earned two sixes — perfect marks — and was placed first by eight of the nine judges. Canada had never before won a world figure skating title.

Canada's newest sweetheart returned home a national heroine and was royally feted, especially in Ottawa, her hometown, which showed its gratitude with the gift of a canary yellow Buick convertible. Two months later, she was forced to give it back because the International Olympic Committee said the gift violated the amateur code. In Prague the next winter, she successfully defended her European title, and then on terrible, slushy outdoor ice in St. Moritz, her event postponed and almost moved elsewhere because of the melting conditions, she won the Olympic gold medal, affirming not only her superior skating ability but also her grit and determination. She capped off that incredible European trip of 1948 by again winning the world title in Davos, Switzerland. "She is a thoroughbred," gushed a Montreal sportswriter, "the sort of person who comes along once in a life time to enable and glorify sport, erasing much of the dross that surrounds it."

Barbara Ann first learned to skate during the late 1930s at the prestigious Minto Skating Club in Ottawa. Still very young (she was eleven in 1940), there was no need for her to turn profes-

sional during the war, unlike other top Canadian skaters of this time, who were forced to pursue their careers with shows like the Ice Follies and Ice Capades if they wanted to skate at all.

Mary Rose Thacker, for example, from the Winnipeg Winter Club, won the Canadian senior ladies' title in 1939, 1941 and 1942, and was North American champion in 1940 and 1941. Trained by the best coaches in New York and London, skating and performing since she was four years old, she was also an expert swimmer and horsewoman, had studied ballet, dancing and fencing, and spoke several languages. A "pretty girl, sweet and shy" with brown hair and hazel eyes — quite small in stature at five feet four inches and

Barbara Ann Scott winning the 1947 World Figure Skating Championships in Stockholm.

Barbara Ann Scott, photographed by Yousef Karsh.
Below: The Reliable Toy Company was quick to recognize the marketability of a Barbara Ann Scott doll, and sold them from 1949 to 1955 in a variety of costumes.

115 pounds — she was portrayed as a "symphony on skates," a "will o' the wisp" and "graceful as a melody." Many predicted Thacker would capture the world titles; i-n fact, she was named to the 1940 team for an Olympics that did not take place. She had no choice but to turn professional, and after a brief stint performing in ice shows, applied her talents to coaching.

Norah McCarthy, a "beautiful black-haired skating cutie," was a nineteen-year-old star in the famous Ice Follies, touring all over North America and making a great deal of money. She had become a professional in 1942, having won the Canadian senior ladies' amateur championship in 1940, the pairs title (with Ralph McCreath) in 1939 and 1940, and the same North American championship in 1941. Norah, and her younger sister Tasie, had been skating since childhood. They were devastated when their father, a railway official, was transferred to North Bay, Ontario, because that city lacked a skating coach, but their mother brought them to Ottawa each winter to skate and train at the Minto Club. In summertime, the McCarthy sisters trained in the United States at the skating school in Lake Placid, often starring in the glitzy carnivals put on especially for tourists. Skating for eight months a year meant for the most part they were tutored privately. It all paid off. In 1938, Norah won the Canadian junior ladies' title, as did Tasie the following year. After winning the senior championship two years later, Norah was named to the 1940 Olympic team. Like Mary Rose Thacker before her, she was forced to become a professional in order to pursue a skating career.

As a gangling teenager Eleanor O'Meara won her first singles skating title at the Toronto Granite Club in 1931. Five years later she vaulted into the senior ranks, stealing the senior Canadian title from Constance (Wilson) Samuel, the perpetual winner for over a decade. She did it again in 1938, but lost out to Mary Rose Thacker and Norah McCarthy in the next few years. In 1941, Eleanor teamed up with husky six-foot Ralph McCreath (as did McCarthy before her), and together they won both the Canadian and the North American senior pairs title. Described by a journalist as the "pretty, long-legged Canadian girl, with the flashing smile and freckled brow," Eleanor turned down many offers to skate professionally until the spring of 1943, when she signed with the Ice Capades. An immediate success, O'Meara was considered by some enthusiasts as the "greatest natural skating ballerina" — greater even, according to a California columnist, than the legendary Sonja Henie.

Canadian figure skaters were forced to turn professional during wartime because amateur competitions were cancelled, and many skated with the Ice Follies and Ice Capades.

Figure skating, and the possibility of stardom in an ice show represented a dream for many young Canadian girls, especially those whose parents could afford the skating lessons, special coaches and travel to competitions. By 1946, 20 percent of the Ice Capades' cast was Canadian, and many more were considered in the frequent auditions seeking new talent. Soon after her Olympic glory, Barbara Ann Scott turned professional, a glamorous if somewhat reluctant celebrity, eventually replacing her own idol, Sonja Henie, in the Hollywood Ice Revue. At her peak, she earned over $100,000 a year, not just from skating but also from lucrative product endorsements of skates, clothing, dolls and other products like Canada Dry ginger ale, making her the first woman athlete in Canada to be transformed from a celebrity to a commodity.

The immediate postwar period of women's sport in Canada was characterized by a remarkable emphasis on beauty, grace, femininity and, for some athletes, glamour. Gone for the most part were debates about whether or not sport would masculinize women competitors, because the proof was there for all to see: so long as women participated in "beauty producing" sports like figure skating, synchronized swimming or gymnastics, and so long as they looked feminine

on the tennis or badminton courts, golf courses and ski hills, they would not be criticized.

Skiing twins Rhona and Rhoda Wurtele, for instance, whose careers had been affected by the war, were media favourites. A wartime issue of *True Comics*, which chronicled the deeds of notable men and women, featured the twins, claiming they were "two of the world's best

AT THE AGE OF TWENTY-ONE, THE WURTELE TWINS OF CANADA ARE TWO OF THE WORLD'S BEST WOMEN SKIERS AND PROBABLY THE BEST ALL-AROUND ATHLETES CANADA HAS EVER PRODUCED.

Media favourites Rhona and Rhoda Wurtele were members of the 1948 Winter Olympic team.

women skiers and probably the best all-round athletes Canada has ever produced" (obviously *True Comics* was unaware of Bobbie Rosenfeld, voted Canada's woman athlete of the half-century.). Both Rhona and Rhoda were members of the 1948 Winter Olympic team competing in St. Moritz, but, due to a disastrous training accident, Rhoda did not compete, and Rhona fell twice during her downhill race, coming last. Both married in 1949 and continued to compete, which was unusual. Rhoda competed well into the 1950s, and was a member of the 1952 Olympic team, earning a ninth place in the giant slalom.

The long wartime period had disrupted the entire society, especially the social-sexual order — the pattern of relations between men and women and what it meant to be masculine or feminine. Although the war provided many Canadian women with opportunities for travel, work and responsibility, and temporarily caused a destabilization in the traditional sexual division of labour, it also reinforced traditional notions of womanhood and femininity. With the Allied victory in Europe in the spring of 1945, weary veterans returned home to be greeted with admiration and gratitude by their government and the general public alike. Men, and especially male veterans, were given preference in employment; women were encouraged by government and industry to return home and stay there. The idealized women's life changed dramatically from one of employment and productivity during the war (while at the same time taking care of the home front) to an emphasis immediately after the war on domesticity and raising children (of the postwar baby boom).

High-profile women athletes in this era contributed to and strengthened the prevailing social-sexual order in several ways. Strength, muscles and beauty were strangely incompatible, and when all were present, femininity and

A wartime recruiting poster featuring the Canadian Women's Army Corps.

womanliness needed to be constantly reaffirmed. The *Canadian Sport Monthly*, which in the 1950s was the official magazine for golf, skiing, tennis and badminton, frequently ran photos of comely women athletes in bathing suits (sand skiing for instance), prompting one male reader to compliment them for their "cheesecake."

But athletes sweating on the basketball courts, softball pitches, ice hockey rinks and cinder tracks were suspect, their femininity (and increasingly their sexuality) continually questioned. The public was assured, over and over again, that those who achieved success were feminine and womanly, and when their competitive

Jackie MacDonald was Canada's best shot put and discus thrower in the 1950s.

days were over, they would glide happily into married domesticity and fulfill their natural responsibility to have children. The exceptions were unusual and few.

Jackie MacDonald — tall, statuesque, glamorous, and frequently compared to actress Marilyn Monroe — was one such exception. As a twenty-year-old elementary school teacher, having been a good athlete in high school, she had begun working with Lloyd Percival, who in the early 1940s started the Sports College in Toronto and was well known throughout the country for his Saturday morning radio show providing training and fitness tips. He was impressed by this vivacious bleach-blonde who regularly arrived at practice on a Harley-Davidson motorcycle and was determined to be the best shot put and discus thrower in the world.

Jackie started by winning the Canadian shot put title in 1953 and was named to the 1954 British Empire and Commonwealth Games team. She did well in the shot put competition, coming second and establishing a new Canadian record, and was all set to compete in the discus when suddenly, just before her event, she was withdrawn by the Canadian officials for alleged "professionalism." Her picture had appeared in a soft drink advertisement in a Vancouver paper, although Jackie herself gained nothing financially from the appearance. The stodgy Canadian track and field officials, intent on upholding the "amateur" ideal, were upset over the fact that Percival made his living from coaching and that his leading-edge techniques were gaining attention; this was a way to damage his credibility. She was cleared a few days after the Games ended and competed a few months later at the 1955 Pan-American Games in Mexico, coming fifth in the discus (there was no shot put event).

Far more crucial to Jackie in the 1950s was her image as the best woman shot putter this side of the Iron Curtain, obviously muscular and strong yet claiming fragility and femininity. Coach Percival wanted her to bulk up significantly, to become even more muscular, and Jackie not only had reservations, she was more concerned about becoming some sort of "freak." June Callwood wrote a feature article for *Maclean's* that stressed Jackie's many attempts to confront her "Amazon in shorts and spikes" image:

By dressing with delicacy, she vigorously combats the effects of being able to lift a hundred-and-fifty-pound bell bar. She lightens her hair to honey blonde, wears sooty mascara and flowerlike perfumes, favors slender-heeled pumps, pastel sweaters, pearls and dangling earrings. As her muscles grow stronger, she fights back with an angora beret, sewn with sequins. Though she is tall — five feet ten and weighing a hundred and sixty pounds — Jackie is determined never to be picked out of a crowd as the girl most likely to move a piano.

The article was accompanied by a series of photos showing Jackie weight training and competing, but also as a grade-school teacher, preparing for a date, sewing curtains, and "aproned, domestic and very, very feminine."

Mary "Bonnie" Baker began playing softball in a Regina city league at age twelve as a catcher. Married at seventeen, she worked in the Army and Navy department store during the day and played ball for the company-sponsored team a couple of times a week. By 1943 she was scouted by the All-American Girls Professional Baseball League and signed to play for South Bend, promising her soldier husband, on active duty overseas, she would quit the moment the war ended. Of more than 600 women who played in the All-American, 64 were Canadian; the majority came from the Prairies, especially Saskatchewan. At its peak, the league had expanded to ten cities throughout the United States, and drew hundreds of thousands of fans.

Concerned about the tarnished, "mannish" image of women's softball, the All-American adopted the rules of men's baseball since the fans, a good percentage being male, would be drawn to feminine and attractive women playing a man's game. "The more feminine the appearance of the performer, the more dramatic the performance," intoned the league handbook, which unequivocally stipulated how the players were to dress off the field (no shorts, slacks, jeans or anything "masculine"), wear their hair (off the shoulder but no boyish bobs), apply cosmetics (always use lipstick), and behave in public (no smoking, drinking, obscene language or "moral lapses"). Their playing uniform consisted of a belted tunic dress with short sleeves that buttoned up the front left side, coloured in pastel

Three Canadian All-American Girls. From left, Eleanor Callow, Olive Little and Mary Baker.

shades of green, blue, yellow or peach. Mary Baker's well-groomed style and dark good looks established her as the embodiment of the All-American virtues, and she was often chosen by the league to pose for publicity shots and act as a spokesperson.

Eleanor "Squirt" Callow from Winnipeg, a solid fielder who played for the Rockford Peaches from 1948 to 1954, became the Babe Ruth of the league, with more home runs and triples than any other player in the league's history. Others had their moment of glory — like Olive "Ollie" (Bend) Little of the Moose Jaw Royals, an original member of the Rockford Peaches, who pitched the first no-hitter in league history.

The All-American came to an end in 1954. The war had delivered a captive audience eager for entertainment in bleak times, but postwar prosperity brought a renewed interest in men's professional sport enhanced by television's ability to bring live games into millions of homes. The league became more out of step with the times, especially with regard to the domestic role of women in the 1950s.

Softball, however, continued to grow and expand. The first Dominion women's

The Vancouver Hedlunds basketball team became the team to beat after the demise of the Edmonton Grads in 1940.

championship was held during the 1951 Canadian National Exhibition, with Edmonton Mortons beating Toronto Ace Bowling in a best-of-three series. The CNE was also responsible for bringing the women's "world" championship, sponsored by the Amateur Softball Association of America, to Toronto in both 1952 and 1953. Several Canadian teams entered the tournament each year but they were eventually eliminated by the stronger American teams.

Women's ice hockey, unfortunately, did not flourish. After the war, male leagues were given priority on the public and community ice arenas, especially to accommodate the growth of minor league hockey for boys. When nine-year-old Abby Hoffman begged her parents to let her play organized hockey in the mid-fifties, she was (unknown to the league) the only girl among 400 boys. When it was discovered that "Ab," the 73-pound defence stalwart for the St. Catharines Tee Pees, was a girl, everyone was taken totally by surprise. Abby had honed her hockey skills on the streets and rink near her home, and she desperately wanted to play in a proper league. Her parents went along with the deception so she could play, taking her to the hockey rinks fully dressed. Abby, who later went on to have a stellar athletic career as a middle distance runner, was a media celebrity for a short while, and there were hopes that a girls' league could be organized in Toronto, but the interest was simply not there.

With little public or media interest in women's hockey, teams had increasing difficulty finding sponsors. Often it was softball players looking for an exciting winter sport who tried to generate interest in the game. Even in the universities, where women's hockey had a long and distinguished past, interest dwindled, and so did the finances to support the teams. Dominion championships were held, at least during the early part of the decade, but the teams competing were those who could find sponsorship to travel.

Women's basketball was also struggling, although it was much stronger in some areas of the country than others. Western teams dominated because they had always played men's rules and were used to a faster, more complex game, whereas players in eastern Canada were brought up on girls' rules in the schools and universities and were more comfortable with a slower, less demanding and aggressive game. With the demise of the Edmonton Grads in 1940, the Vancouver Hedlunds became the team to beat. They won the Canadian senior women's basketball championships between 1942 and 1946, although due to wartime travel restrictions, the championship was only challenged by other teams in the West. Even after the war, national champions in basketball were declared after a series of Eastern and Western playoffs, with the Manitoba-Ontario border serving as the national divide. The provincial champions from the two furthest provinces would travel east or west to the next province, play the champion there, and then move on to the next province if they won, or return home if they lost.

Chapter Six

FAVOURITE DAUGHTERS AND COMPETING MOTHERS

Seventeen-year-old golfer Marlene Stewart from Fonthill, rated the top athlete in Ontario in 1951, was often described as a pert teenager, a bright-eyed miss with a ready smile, or the freckled-faced Little Miss Stewart. Barely over five feet tall, she was often called a child, since her achievements seemed all the more notable given her diminutive stature. Depicted by sportswriter Trent Frayne as the "chattiest, cheeriest, chirpiest kid-next-door who ever snapped her bubblegum in the high-school gymnasium," she astounded the experts by winning the Ontario ladies' golf championship (knocking off veteran Ada MacKenzie), as well as both the Canadian Ladies' Closed and Open amateur championships.

By 1957, Marlene had twice been awarded the Lou Marsh Trophy as Canada's outstanding athlete, as well as the Velma Springstead Trophy, and for four years (1952, 1953, 1956, 1957) she was voted the top woman athlete by the Canadian sports press. She had won four Canadian Open and six Canadian Closed championships, plus the British and the United States titles, all in the space of six years. According to the pundits, her future choices were simple — marriage or professional golf — and if the former, it "would see the end of her winning stature." Canada's favourite daughter was married in April 1957, but she continued to play tournament golf for a year or so, after which she took three years off to have two children. As Marlene Stewart Streit, she returned to competition in 1963 and again won the Canadian Closed and Open championships against a new crop of women golfers including Gail Harvey (later

Moore), Betty Stanhope Cole, Judy Darling (later Evans), and Gayle Hitchens (later Borthwick), dispelling any doubts about whether she could have succeeded professionally had she chosen that route. That same year she was awarded the Bobbie Rosenfeld trophy for the fifth time as Canada's outstanding woman athlete.

Marlene Stewart Streit, who still competes today, has been Canada's most successful amateur woman golfer.

Betty Stanhope Cole, still active today, is Alberta's most successful woman golfer, having competed at the local, provincial, national and international levels.

Marilyn Bell at 16, in a photo she autographed for Gus Ryder, her trainer and coach.

A predominant image of Canadian women athletes in the 1950s was that of anybody's daughter, the girl next door with special talent, whom all would be proud to claim — providing she was white, Anglo-Saxon, and preferably from English Canada. These were wholesome, normal girls, the sort parents liked their sons to date and eventually marry. Indeed, they did get married, sometimes in the middle of successful athletic careers, which frequently brought an end to competition, but in some cases only a brief hiatus while they produced several children. Thus, another image became firmly established in this era, that of the competing mother, although medical and public opinion were rarely on her side.

Three years younger, marathon swimmer Marilyn Bell had much in common with Marlene Stewart. Only teenagers when they first came to prominence, both were from middle-class families. Marlene's father owned an electrical appliance store on Fonthill's main street, and the family lived behind the store. Marilyn's father was a grocery store buyer, and due to the shortage of postwar housing in Toronto, his family lived in an apartment over the store; her mother had been a stenographer before their marriage. Both athletes had one younger sister.

When Marlene was twelve, like the boys with whom she skated, skied and played ball, she started caddying at the Lookout Point golf club

Alex Gibb presenting Marilyn Bell with the Lou Marsh Trophy in 1954, with Gus Ryder in the background and an unidentified swimmer on the left.

near her home, saving up enough money to buy her own clubs. Gordon McInnes, the club's pro, rewarded his tireless caddie by showing her how to hit a golf ball and patiently correcting her faults. She entered her first tournament in 1949. That same year, twelve-year-old Marilyn came second in the CNE junior one-mile swim. Her mother enjoyed swimming and had prompted her young daughter to take lessons. When it became clear that Marilyn preferred distance swimming over sprints, she came under the tutelage of Gus Ryder at the Lakeshore Swimming Club, where some of the best marathon swimmers in Canada trained. At fourteen, Marilyn turned professional in order to earn money for university, winning $300 in 1952 when she came fourth in the women's three-mile CNE swim. The following year she came third and added $500 to her bank account.

Marilyn was all set to compete in the 1954 CNE marathon swim, when both the women's and men's events were cancelled. In their place, the CNE signed a highly publicized $10,000 agreement with thirty-four year-old American marathoner Florence Chadwick, giving her $2,500 in advance with the rest to be awarded if she completed a swim across Lake Ontario. Earlier in July, Marilyn had competed (and won $1,150) in her first major marathon swim, coming seventh overall as the first woman to finish the 26-mile Atlantic City ocean marathon around Absecon Island. More determined than ever to tackle Lake Ontario, and also the famous Chadwick, Marilyn sought sponsorship

A young Marlene Stewart in action.

(through Alex Gibb) from the *Toronto Star*. CNE officials relented on the condition she swim "for the glory of Canada," refusing to guarantee any prize money if she was successful.

With no live television to record the swim itself, begun late at night on September 3 from Youngstown in New York, and no way to keep track of the swimmers except through sporadic press reports, many were surprised the next night, when after swimming forty miles in twenty-one hours, Marilyn touched the concrete breakwater at Toronto's Sunnyside. Florence Chadwick, exhausted and sick from the rolling swells, had been pulled out several hours earlier.

Canada's "little lady of the Lake" was feted and honoured unlike any woman athlete who had gone before. There was a ticker-tape parade and celebration in Toronto; interviews with *Time*, *Life* and numerous other magazines; and 25,000 requests to the *Toronto Star* for a free photo of Marilyn. She accumulated gifts, prizes, and contracts worth $50,000, and made countless radio, television and personal appearances throughout Ontario. There was talk of movie stardom, but in the end, Marilyn Bell decided to return to her studies at Loretto College School, train for future swims, and continue to teach swimming at the Lakeshore Swimming Club.

On July 31, 1955, she became the youngest person (at seventeen) to swim the English Channel. The following summer she attempted to cross the Juan de Fuca Strait from Victoria on Vancouver Island to Port Angeles on the United States side — regarded as the Mount Everest of marathon swimming — but failed. Barely conscious after battling the cold, rough waters for nearly ten hours, she was pulled out. She tried again in a few weeks, this time swimming from Port Angeles to Victoria, and succeeded in 11 hours, 35 minutes, becoming only the fifth swimmer and second woman to swim the Strait. In 1957, like Marlene Stewart Streit a few months before her, Canada's other favourite daughter got married. But unlike her contemporary, Marilyn moved to the United States, giving up swimming and her university studies to devote her energies to marriage, domesticity and starting a family.

Marlene and Marilyn differed in the end. The golfer remained an amateur and competed all her life — still today in senior tournaments — whereas the swimmer became a professional at an early age and ended her career after just a few years, so that she is remembered as she was in the mid-

1950s: a "sweet, normal Canadian girl" who did something truly remarkable.

There was another swimmer, along with Marilyn Bell and Florence Chadwick, in the waters of Lake Ontario that cold, dark night in September 1954. Winnie Roach Leuszler, a twenty-eight-year-old mother of three, has been written out of that story so many times, it is important to tell it here. Unlike the privileged "favourite daughters," she was a working-class, competing mother. Winnie made her professional swimming debut in 1947, just two months after the birth of her first child, when she competed in the women's five-mile swim at the CNE because she needed the prize money. She placed second, winning $1,000. She repeated the feat in 1948, coming third, although this time she was three months pregnant with her second child (revealed after she climbed out of the water). Constantly told by race officials she should not be swimming, she had ignored them, gotten a doctor's approval, and gone ahead anyway. By the early 1950s, Winnie was rated as one of the top marathon swimmers in the world.

The English Channel beckoned, so she convinced the Toronto *Telegram* to sponsor her trip (one-way) across the Atlantic for the second international race in 1951. Bad weather delayed

Greeted by some 350,000 well-wishers in Toronto, Marilyn Bell was feted with a ticker tape parade.

the swim for several days, but on August 16 a flotilla of small ships accompanied the swimmers across the waters from Cap Gris Nez in France to the Dover port on the English side. She finished the swim in 13 hours, 45 minutes, the second woman in the race and the seventh overall, and, most significant of all, the first Canadian ever to swim the Channel. Her prize

Winnie Roach Leuszler, a mother of three, was the first Canadian to swim the English Channel in 1951.

Irene MacDonald was Canada's best springboard diver in the 1950s.

money amounted to about $1,400, out of which she paid her own and her father Eddie's way home (he always coached her). They arrived back to a ticker-tape parade up Bay Street in Toronto, where, at City Hall, she was presented with a silver tea service. "Winnie is a real champion," declared the mayor.

Now a celebrity, Winnie toured with a water show that travelled to various cities in Canada and the United States. Her mother looked after her children and her career soldier husband put food on the table. The decision to swim Lake Ontario in 1954 came more by chance than planning, and she was not sponsored in any way. In the dark and confusion at the start, she soon lost contact with her guide boat, turned back, and was picked up by a fisherman who returned her to shore. She started again the following morning, but with the water churning she suffered cramps after swimming nearly two-thirds of the way, and she too was pulled out. She made two more attempts to cross that lake, once in July 1956, when she was pulled out after eighteen hours, and again a few weeks later as an unofficial entry in a CNE-sponsored swim, but this time she lasted only three hours.

Often described in the media as pert, wee, dainty, petite and, on one occasion, "fresh-as-dew little mermaid," swimmer Helen Stewart from Vancouver was in reality five feet seven inches in height, a solid 135 pounds, and still growing. Her best year was in 1955 when in March at the Pan-Am Games she won a gold medal in the 100-metre freestyle. While professional swimmers grabbed most of the headlines during the fifties, Canada's amateur swimmers, especially the women, were equally talented and successful, mostly because of the establishment of proper training and coaching regimes. Beth Whitall from Montreal was the star performer at the 1955 Pan-Ams, winning both the 400-metre freestyle and the 100-metre butterfly; Lenore Fisher of Ocean Falls, British Columbia, took the 100-metre backstroke. At the 1956 Melbourne Olympics, several swimmers reached the finals of their events, including Virginia Grant from Toronto, Sara Barber of Brantford, Ontario, and Beth Whittall. The 400-metre relay team finished fifth, and diver Irene MacDonald came third in the 3-metre event. Canada was at last approaching a "world power" in women's swimming.

Lucile Wheeler was the first Canadian ever to win a skiing medal at an Olympics (in 1956). Her family owned a resort lodge in the Laurentians in Quebec, where she learned to ski at an early age. At twelve she won the Canadian junior championships, at fourteen she was a member of the Canadian team competing at the world championships, and at sixteen she was the youngest Olympian on the 1952 Canadian team. Winters spent in Europe, and her own talent and determination, made her a world-class skier; her triumphs culminating in the giant slalom and

In 1956, Lucile Wheeler became the first Canadian to win a skiing medal at an Olympic Games.

downhill titles at the world championships in 1958. "She might have been anyone's daughter," wrote the editors of *Canadian Sport Monthly* in their tribute, failing to note Lucile's privileged background and the unique opportunities she had been afforded. Her father estimated that her training and travel had cost him at least $30,000 over the years, which seems like a pittance now but was a good deal of money then. She retired in 1959, acknowledging that the arduous career of a world champion skier would not mix with marriage and children.

Other top skiers, like Joanne Hewson, Rosemarie Schutz, Monique Langlais, Carlyn

Anne Heggtveit was the first Canadian to win an Olympic gold medal in the slalom in 1956. Her skis are shown below.

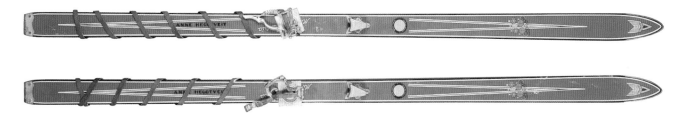

Kruger, Gigi Sequin, Nancy and Janet Holland, Faye Pitt, Claire Monaghan and the incomparable Anne Heggtveit, enjoyed considerable media attention and public support. Brought up in a skiing family in Ottawa, Anne was just a shy youngster when, at fifteen, she surprised everyone by winning the prestigious 1954 Holmenkollen giant slalom in Norway over a field of world-class skiers. A broken leg the next year meant that her performance at the 1956 Cortina Olympics was respectable, but not what it would have been had she been fully recovered. She made up for it at the next Olympics in Squaw Valley by winning a gold medal in the slalom, a first for Canada. She retired after her Olympic victory, marrying a few years later.

The old arguments about strenuous exercise making women unfit for motherhood continued to circulate, especially in sports like track and field, which were still dogged by claims of reproductive damage, physical masculinization and lack of heterosexual appeal. Most sports and physical activity, done moderately, were acceptable to prepare women for motherhood by making them strong and fit, but actual mothers (and worse still, those pregnant) competing, especially at a very high level, was a very different matter. Even the war and the role women played in it, either working in jobs usually reserved for men or facing physical dangers in war-ravaged Britain and Europe, did little to change attitudes towards mothers competing. After the war, these attitudes became more entrenched, but more women were willing to defy them and prove that motherhood, at least physically, had little to do with athletic competition. In fact, it might be an asset.

At the first Summer Olympics following the war, which were held in London in 1948, the most spectacular and successful athlete was a thirty-year-old housewife and mother of two, who was also in the early stages of her third pregnancy. Fanny Blankers-Koen of the Netherlands, nicknamed the "Flying Dutchwoman," won four gold medals — in the 80-, 100- and 200-metre hurdles and the 4x100-metre relay — and perhaps would have won more had she not been prevented from competing in the high jump, long jump and javelin throw by IOC rules limiting her to three individual events. She demonstrated to the world that pregnancy and motherhood had not diminished her athletic ability; she became a role model for women athletes refusing to let childbearing and raising children prevent them from fulfilling their potential.

By the time Doreen Mcleod Ryan was married in 1952 at age twenty-one, she was the best woman speed skater in Canada, indeed in North America. She had come to prominence in 1947

Doreen Ryan combined motherhood and competition to become the top Canadian woman speed skater in the 1950s and early 1960s.

by winning the national junior title, and followed this with winning the intermediate title in 1949 and finally the senior women's Canadian championship first in 1951 and again the following year, when she also won the North American title. Between 1951 and 1964, Doreen won ten senior titles, and competed in both the 1960 Winter Olympics (the first time women's speed

Rosella Thorne, (far right) from the Montreal Olympic Club, was the most accomplished Canadian woman athlete of colour in the 1950s.

though in 1945 Myrtle Cook wondered what all the fuss was about when baseball player Jackie Robinson, the first Black in the major leagues, signed with the Montreal Royals. As she pointed out in her column, women athletes of colour had long since made their mark on the Canadian scene. The most accomplished Black athlete of this decade was Rosella Thorne of the Montreal Olympic Club, an outstanding track athlete who was a member of several international teams. Born in 1930, she attended Commercial High School in Montreal, and first came to prominence at an international indoor track meet in Hamilton in 1949. She was also a good basketball player and a member of the Montreal Meteors, Canadian intermediate champions in 1950, and along with Violet McKenzie was one of two Black players on the team. With money tight, the 1950 British Empire Games team was drastically reduced, but Thorne made the team and went to Auckland, New Zealand, where she competed in the 80-metre hurdles, broad jump and relay. As a result of her achievements that year, Thorne was awarded both the Velma Springstead Trophy and the Montreal *Daily Star* Trophy. She was a member of the 1952 Summer Olympic team in Helsinki and the 1954 British Empire and Commonwealth Games team in Vancouver, after which she retired from competition.

skating was an official event) in Squaw Valley, California, and the 1964 Olympics in Innsbruck, Austria, while during the same period giving birth to three children, in 1953, 1955 and 1960. Admonished by family and friends that strenuous athletic activity would negatively affect her ability to have children, Doreen ignored this advice, and her first two children "just happened." In order to keep training, she would squeeze in an early morning run before her husband and children awoke, get the family going for the day, often go to a part-time job, do her weight training over the noon hour and, during the skating season, take her children to the oval while she trained, sometimes going out for an additional skate after they were in bed. She was encouraged when she learned that the Russian women skaters, who dominated world competitions, were convinced that having children made them stronger.

"Coloured" athletes (sometimes referred to as "dusky") were still very unusual in this era, even

Chapter Seven

UNRECOGNIZED CHAMPIONS AND MEDIA DARLINGS

The Six Nations Reserve near Brantford in south-western Ontario is the largest Aboriginal community in Canada. Women's softball/fastball has been a tradition there since the 1930s, and some teams, like the Ohsweken Mohawk Ladies, were highly successful — they won three Ontario women's intermediate championships in the 1950s and 1960s. Many superb athletes from the reserve, who also played on non-Aboriginal teams, were never recognized by the mainstream media.

Phyllis "Yogi" Bomberry, the nickname reflecting her superb catching ability, was the first ever female recipient of the Tom Longboat Award, given annually (since 1951) to the most outstanding Aboriginal athlete in Canada, male or female, which she won in 1968. She was catcher for the Toronto Carpetland Senior A team, who won the Canadian senior women's softball championships in 1967 and 1968. She was also a member of the gold medal–winning team at the Canada Games in 1969.

Bev Beaver won numerous top pitcher and most valuable player awards during more than thirty years (1961–1994) of competitive fastball. In 1979, for example, she was named best pitcher, top batter and most valuable player at the Canadian Native championship in Kelowna, as well as all-star pitcher at the North American Native Ladies championship in Saskatoon. In winter, Bev switched to her favourite sport, ice hockey, which she also played competitively for nearly three decades. Awarded the regional Tom Longboat medal in 1967, as the outstanding Native athlete in Ontario, Bev was recognized nationally in 1980, when she also won the Tom Longboat Award.

Women's team sports, like volleyball, basketball, ice hockey, softball, field hockey and others, were flourishing in the 1960s and 1970s, but there was almost total lack of press coverage. Aside from men's professional sports, the sports media were

Phyllis Bomberry was the first female recipient of the Tom Longboat Award, given annually to the most outstanding Aboriginal athlete in Canada.

Twins Sharon and Shirley Firth from Inuvik were the first Canadians to compete in the women's cross-country skiing events at the Olympics (in 1972).

was a member of the 1967 Pan-Am volleyball team. In 1970, when she was in her early forties, she was a member of the Commonwealth Games badminton team.

Identical twins Sharon and Shirley Firth grew up in Aklavik in a traditional Native family, which lived off the land and was then relocated to Inuvik in the Northwest Territories. Introduced to skiing as young teenagers in 1965, the twins were soon coached by a Norwegian hired by the Canadian Amateur Ski Association to find and train the best skiers in the MacKenzie Delta. The Firth sisters — along with Roseanne Allen, also of Inuvik, and Helen Sander from Ontario — were the first Canadians to compete in women's cross-country events at the Olympics (in 1972 in Sapporo, Japan). The Firths and Roseanne were also the first Canadian Aboriginal women to compete in an Olympic Games. Sharon and Shirley went on to win a combined forty-eight Canadian championships, and to compete in three more consecutive Olympics.

riveted on individual athletes, especially those who performed well or, better still, who brought glory to themselves and to Canada by winning an Olympic medal or world championship. In less prestigious events, and certainly in team sports, top athletes were generally ignored.

Marjory Shedd of Toronto was a good example of one such athlete. In the 1940s, she played junior basketball and in 1950 led the Toronto Montgomery Maids to the national senior title. She switched to badminton and volleyball, winning six national singles titles and fourteen ladies' doubles titles in the former. She played on volleyball teams like the champion University Settlement Blacks and

Also making their mark in this era were an increasing number of adventurous women athletes who challenged, and sometimes transgressed, gender roles. In 1960, Toronto secretary Elaine McCrossan was the first Canadian woman, and among the first in North America, to achieve a black belt in judo, symbol of the highest degree of accomplishment.

WOMAN DRIVER!
All about the great girls who race cars

In 1966, Stephanie Ruys de Perez was one of the very few women sports car racers in Canada.

Stephanie Ruys de Perez, a Toronto mother of two whose husband also raced, was one of six serious female sports car racers in Canada in the early 1970s. She drove for the Comstock Racing Team — Canada's first commercially sponsored team. "It's a shock to see a driver remove the helmet," observed one sportswriter, "and shake out a tumble of women's hair."

Women also took up dangerous sports like scuba diving and parachute jumping, but they were still sometimes thwarted in their efforts to cross gender boundaries, even in sports with little risk. In 1966, Abby Hoffman, then a University of Toronto student and aspiring Olympian, attempted on three separate occasions to use the large indoor track in the male-only athletic facilities at Hart House and was refused each time.

Yet, despite the criticism and negative publicity, some women pursued their sporting interests in so-called men's sports. The Canadian Belles, for example, were a group of "rough-and-tough ladies," who were the only team from Canada playing in a four-team women's professional football league in the early 1970s. Originally created as entertainment ("a comedy sport") to be hired out by groups wishing to raise money, the league became highly competitive, but did not last long. Professional roller derby, racing at breakneck speed on roller skates around a track

The Canadian Belles played in a four-team women's professional football league in the early 1970s.

trying to upend opponents, was popular in the United States during the 1960s and 1970s (it is currently making a comeback). One star on the circuit was Francine Cochu from Montreal, who played for the Oakland Bay Bombers, earning about $10,000 playing four or five times a week, ten months of the year.

During the 1960s and 1970s, Canadian women athletes won more world-class championships and captured more individual titles than did Canada's male athletes. Taking into account that the number of events for men was approximately twice that for women at major international games, they outperformed their male counterparts at nearly all these games; they consistently won a greater proportion of medals

at these competitions than would be expected given their much smaller numbers on teams.

Despite these accomplishments, the male sports media tended to excuse the relatively lesser performance of Canada's male amateur athletes either because their talent pool had been depleted through the attraction of professional sport, or because they needed to put childish pursuits aside and get on with the serious business of training for a career and supporting a family. Canadian parents, particularly those with few financial worries, still subscribed to the "Daddy's Little Girl" theory of raising children. Where boys were expected to rush through their schooling and become financially independent as soon as possible, with professional sport as an option if they had talent, there was no great rush to push Canadian girls to independence; besides, there were few opportunities for them in professional sport.

With the exception of golf and tennis, where they could earn money, the only avenue for women to reach the highest pinnacle of their sport was through a medal at a world championship or major international games such as the Olympics, the Pan-American Games, or the British Empire and Commonwealth Games. Certainly in the late 1950s and early 1960s, they got to these international events and trained for them because they had supportive families who could afford to pay. All this changed quite dramatically in a relatively short period of time.

Government involvement in amateur sport from the 1960s onwards resulted in the restructuring and professionalization of the Canadian sport system, as well as radically altering the experience of being a high-performance athlete. Basically, the intensity of training and coaching of young athletes increased markedly, a nascent sports science was applied more rationally, and there were substantially more resources available to bring in top-level coaches (often from Europe) and to provide international competitive opportunities.

At the 1966 British Empire and Commonwealth Games in Jamaica, for example, almost every Canadian athlete reached the finals of their event, and the medal totals were higher than ever before, with the most improvement in swimming and on the track. Elaine Tanner, the fifteen-year-old Canadian swimming sensation, accounted for one silver and three gold medals on her own, along with a first and second in the relays, one of which set a world record. It was the best Canadian team showing since the 1930s.

Nancy Greene, Canada's pre-eminent skier in the 1960s, never had a "private" coach, nor paid her way anywhere, because someone always

Swimmer Elaine Tanner was dubbed "Mighty Mouse" by her Vancouver Dolphin teammates.

helped: "I am totally a product of organized skiing in Canada." In 1961, her first year on the European circuit, the best racers in Canada were not necessarily skiers on the national team, but rather those with wealthy parents or from well-to-do ski clubs who could afford to send them abroad. In Nancy's case, it was the citizens of Rossland, her hometown in British Columbia, who raised sufficient capital to send her and another skier to Europe. She and other western-based skiers fought hard to establish a proper program where the national team, composed of only the best skiers chosen through selection trials, was centralized and skiers could coordinate their schooling and skiing. By the time her future husband, Al Raine, took over the program in 1968, it included a large coaching staff and a $600,000 annual budget, of which $150,000 was designated for the national team.

The tone and tenor of how high-profile women athletes were portrayed by Canadian sportswriters also changed considerably. The

Nancy Greene, nicknamed "Tiger," was Canada's pre-eminent skier in the 1960s.

most significant change was that these articles were written almost exclusively by men. Women sports journalists had disappeared from the daily newspapers along with their columns. Bobbie Rosenfeld was still at the *Globe and Mail*, but she was not in good health (she retired in 1966 and died three years later). Myrtle Cook McGowan continued writing for the *Montreal Star*, although less about women's sports, until her retirement in 1969. Women sports writers did not show up again in the sports departments of major Canadian newspapers, and then only in a select few, until well into the 1970s, and they were certainly not employed to write exclusively about women's sport.

The athletes featured and discussed were invariably from individual sports, because, for the most part, international competition for females was still restricted to competitive and synchronized swimming, track and field, skiing, figure skating, gymnastics and fencing. Limited international competition was available in volleyball and basketball, but team athletes were generally ignored by the media. Athletes in individual sports were consistently younger than the international-level athletes of earlier decades, making their accomplishments all the more remarkable. Male sports journalists in Canada, writing about these young athletes in newspapers and magazines, generally treated them with respect, although often paternalistically, like proud fathers beaming over their children's accomplishments.

As young, mostly pre-pubescent teenagers, the athletes were portrayed as androgenous, sometimes boyish, and often impish; their sexuality, established or developing, was never discussed. Halifax swimmer Nancy Garapick, for example, was described as "neither tomboyish, nor overtly feminine; she admits to liking boys, dancing, movies and her 10-speed bike." Sixteen-year-old swimmer Mary Stewart, who a few months before had set a world record in the 110-yard butterfly event, became "a lissome, bubbling youngster with braids in her hair, bands on her teeth and pure magic in her water style." Track star Abby Hoffman, who was fifteen at the time, was depicted in a similar way: "she walks a little like a second baseman and she runs with the fury of a man, she may not be quite so tomboyish as this may sound, but a shy and pleasant teenage girl."

Some questioned whether it was reasonable to expect such young teenagers to withstand the pressures of their own dreams — often unrealistic given the rising standards of international competition — let alone those of an entire nation. At the Mexico City Olympics in 1968, under enormous pressure to bring back gold, swimmer Elaine Tanner came second in her best events, the 100- and 200-metre backstroke, and picked up a bronze as a member of the 4x100-metre freestyle relay team. Even though this was the best-ever performance at an Olympics by a Canadian swimming team, the seventeen-year-old Tanner was devastated by what she, and some members of the Canadian press, viewed as failure, which prompted her to retire from competition the following year.

Nancy Garapick set a world record in 1975 when she was only thirteen, and was expected to bring back gold at the 1976 Olympics in Montreal. "To Canada," observed one sportswriter, "Nancy is one of those Great White Hopes that every nation seizes upon in the year before the Olympics." She finished with a bronze in both the 100- and 200-metre backstroke, and an Olympic record set in one of the heats for the 100-metre, yet was immediately grilled by the media about why she hadn't won. Much later, the two East German swimmers who beat Nancy admitted to using performance-enhancing drugs.

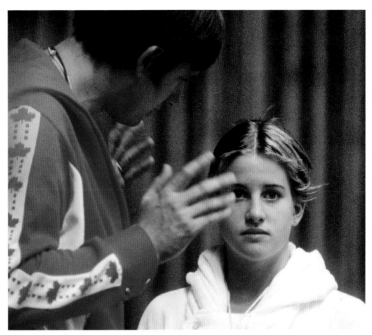

Swimmer Nancy Garapick being prepped by her coach at the Montreal Olympics in 1976.

Although admiration for the youngsters was sometimes patronizing and often tinged with paternalism, more mature women athletes were not always treated with as much respect. A whole new way of writing about high-profile women athletes, mostly in their twenties, emerged in the 1960s. The two most obvious changes were the explicit, sexualized descriptions of their physical appearance and their treatment as sex objects. What was only hinted at in the immediate post-war period became far more conspicuous, the language more candid, and the innuendo regarding sexuality more daring. Male sports journalists rarely refrained from commenting upon the "womanliness" of their subjects, as if to confirm their own manhood and heterosexuality.

Where earlier sportswriters often maintained that athleticism and femininity were mutually exclusive, the 1960s saw a deliberate attempt to link the two in ways not seen before. The downside was that often an athlete's physical appearance was the focus rather than her accomplishments, and female athletes who were not feminine in a conventional sense, or especially attractive, were cruelly singled out and criticized, also in ways not seen before.

Writing about twenty-one-year-old Jenny Wingerson, one of Canada's first pentathletes (80-metre hurdles, shot put, high jump, long jump and 200-metre sprint), the journalist

Debbie Brill was Canada's best woman high jumper throughout the 1970s and 1980s.

focused on her good looks, making it clear she was the "loveliest" entrant in the women's pentathlon at the 1964 Tokyo Olympics: "[She] is twenty-one, has sunny blonde hair, long shapely legs and honey skin and competes in the world's least likely sport, apart from free-style wrestling, for beautiful girls who want to keep their good looks . . . Russian girls are best at the pentathlon — with their blunt, muscular bodies, they *look* like pentathlon winners."

Debbie Van Kiekebelt, also a pentathlete who competed internationally for Canada in the early 1970s, received this from another observer: "She is a striking woman, and very tall. Except for her thighs, which are athlete-thick, she has the body of a fashion model and, in fact, has dabbled in modelling from time to

time since she was 13, including a Miss Chatelaine magazine cover. She has fountaining brunette hair held fast this morning by a gold bandana. A clear oval face that erupts into lopsided smiles. A modest bosom under her white Olympic T-shirt with its red stripes and maple leaf. And those legs — they seem to go on forever — lithe and shapely in red shorts that keep hiking up."

Debbie Brill, Canada's top high-jumper in 1970 (she had cleared six feet, which was nine inches higher than Ethel Catherwood's 1928 gold medal jump), maintains that the Canadian sports media "discovered" women's track and field at this time because suddenly "there was a bunch of us young, talented and, by and large, quite good-looking." She elaborated:

There was Diane Jones, blonde, confident and so well-stacked that she could walk around the dressing room with a towel knotted under an arm and comfortably supported; there were the sprinters Stephanie Berto and Patty Loverock; long jumper Brenda Eisler, and pentathlete Debbie van Kiekebelt, a particular darling of the Toronto media. There had been a general understanding that track and field women tended to be homely; now, suddenly there was a crop that passed certain tests, both on the track and in front of the cameras.

Being in front of the cameras and being viewed by millions on their television sets was becoming important, especially in women's golf. Twenty-year-old Sandra Post from Oakville, Ontario, stunned the golf world when she defeated the number one American player Kathy Whitworth at the LPGA championship on June 24, 1968, at the Pleasant Valley Country Club in Sutton, Massachusetts. A child prodigy, who had her sights on a professional golf career at an early age, she was by the late 1960s a seasoned player with a strong record in United States tournaments. She was the first Canadian ever to play on the LPGA Tour and went on to win eight more LPGA tournaments.

Yet, despite Sandra's accomplishments and the recognition that she (along with skier Nancy Greene and swimmer Elaine Tanner) was putting Canada back into the prestigious world of international sport, one journalist wrote:

. . . Little Sandra Post, who is five-foot-four, 125 pounds and pretty, pugnacious and confident ('cocky' her manager calls it) and as concerned with finding Mr. Right as she is with becoming the world's greatest lady golfer, tied up her sun-bleached hair in green plastic rollers, chose a blue miniskirt for the morning and went to sleep dreaming about the treachery of that dogleg, par-five 12th hole and her boyfriend Dave, whose

Jocelyne Bourassa played on the LPGA Tour from 1972 to 1979.

golf career has been interrupted by the U.S. Vietnam draft.

The focus was less on Sandra's success and more on how the LPGA was fending off charges that "women athletes are either not women, or at least not womanly" by their determined "miniskirted effort to glamorize girl golfers." We learn more about the LPGA's femininity campaign, and Sandra Post's efforts in that respect, than we do about women's golf.

Karen Magnussen's silver medal at the 1972 Winter Olympics in Sapporo was the only Canadian medal of these Games.

Another top golfer during this era was Jocelyne Bourassa from Shawinigan, Quebec, and the second Canadian to play with the LPGA. Always a crowd-pleaser, she was well into a stellar amateur career when a wealthy Montreal businessman became her sponsor, which allowed her to play on the 1972 LPGA Tour. He also organized a Canadian Ladies' Professional Golf Association, and brought the LPGA Tour to Montreal by sponsoring the $50,000 La Canadienne, held in June 1973. Although everyone hoped Bourassa would win, very few thought she could — but win she did after a sudden-death playoff with two other players. Joycelyn Bourassa was the toast of Shawinigan and the rest of Canada; she went on to play until 1979, when a bad knee forced her to leave the Tour.

According to one sportswriter, Joycelyn "radiated an approachable tomboy charm." He continued: "She's a husky woman, a little broad in the beam, and her face seems slightly smallish for the torso. Her face can't make up its mind whether it belongs to the cute kid next door or to a determined pug, someone with a tough style. It lets you know, anyway, that it is the face of someone independent, aggressive, a woman who can — what the hell — play touch football or baseball with men." It is difficult to tell that this is the same Jocelyne Bourassa described by James Barclay in his superb history of golf in Canada: ". . . a jaunty, dark-haired beauty of five feet five-and-a-half inches, with determined blue eyes and an engaging smile, captured the hearts of many Canadians golfers or not. Very much a product of Quebec — and oh! How it was proud of her — she had the Trevino-like quality of making golf seem fun while playing it with deadly earnestness."

Despite the blatant sexism, most Canadian sportswriters of this era treated women's sport and women athletes seriously, especially those who achieved international success. In 1973, *Homemaker's Magazine* ran a salute to Canada's best women athletes: figure skater Karen Magnussen, equestrian Barbara Simpson Kerr, skier Judy Crawford, divers Bev Boys and Cindy Shatto, track stars Glenda Reiser, Debbie Van Kiekebelt and Abby Hoffman, golfers Sandra Post and Jocelyne Bourassa, tennis player Andrée Martin, badminton expert Nancy McKinley, table tennis star Violetta Nesukaitis, and Olympic swimmer and national team volleyball player Helen (Stewart) Hunt. Most of the country's best athletes were women, argued the author, because "Canadian women have been winning more world-class championships, capturing more individual titles and generally displaying more style than Canada's men have come close to managing in the same time period."

Chapter Eight

FIGHTING FOR GENDER EQUALITY

By the mid-1970s, Abby Hoffman's long and distinguished track career was coming to an end. She competed in one more Olympics (her fourth) in Montreal in 1976, where she was chosen to carry the Canadian flag in the opening ceremonies. Always political, articulate and independent, she was increasingly an outspoken voice for the plight of amateur athletes in Canada, especially women. Through newspaper and magazine articles, radio commentaries and public speaking, like Bobbie Rosenfeld, Alexandrine Gibb, Myrtle Cook and Phyllis Griffiths before her, she took on the male sports media by challenging their sexist and stereotypical portrayals of female athletes; she chastised school systems for neglecting girls' sports and physical education; she raged against the lack of professional opportunities for women athletes; and she condemned the sex inequities of the sports world, especially the lack of recreation programs, facilities, training opportunities and prize money. She marvelled that Canadian women athletes had done so well over the years "despite the apparent conspiracy amongst the schools, the media, the recreation authorities and the Canadian culture itself to turn girls away from sport."

Parents all across the country were waking up to the fact that their daughters were not being treated in the same way as their sons when it came to recreational and sporting opportunities. More importantly, recreation agencies and sport organizations, most of whom were dependent on public facilities and funds, could no longer

sustain the argument that they had no moral or legal obligation to provide equal opportunities to both sexes. Sport-related complaints of sex discrimination began to come to the attention of provincial human rights commissions; the majority of cases involved young girls wishing to play on all-male sports teams, usually at the all-star level. Some human rights commissions refused to accept such complaints, arguing that they did not consider sport and recreation to be within their jurisdiction. In the cases that did go through the full judicial process, the issues they raised were often lost in the legal wrangling over interpretation of the law. The main value of these

Far more Canadian girls play soccer than play ice hockey, and the growth continues to be steady.

Chantal Petitclerc (in red) on her way to a gold medal in the 800-metre at the 2004 Olympics in Athens.

sport-related human rights cases was to bring public interest, concern and pressure to bear on eliminating unequal, sex-discriminatory sport and recreation programs.

Feminist activism in Canadian sport now has a long and rich history. It began in the early 1970s, when a small group of women (and a few men) in sport organizations, governments, schools and universities — all committed to effecting change — organized conferences, wrote reports, mounted legal challenges, founded advocacy organizations, lobbied politicians and government officials or whatever it took to bring

about gender equality. Important now are not the details of this struggle, but whether or not there is gender equality in Canadian sport today. The answer is, of course, yes and no.

On the positive side, there is much to recount. Quietly and often with little media attention, hundreds of Canada's top women athletes have gloriously made their mark on the world stage as many others had done before. Today, they constitute as much as 50 percent (and sometimes more) of the membership of many national teams; they also have equal access to training and competitive environments, as well as health,

Hayley Wickenheiser, Caroline Ouellette and Vicky Sunohara celebrate a Canadian victory at the 2007 IIHF World Women's Championship.

medical and sport science services. At the 2004 Summer Olympics in Athens, 50 percent of Canada's medals and 53 percent of the nation's top eight place finishes were earned by female athletes. At the 2006 Winter Olympics in Torino, Italy, fourteen out of nineteen Canadian medals were won by women, with speed skater Cindy Klassen capturing five of them. Canadian females also accounted for more than half our medals at the winter Paralympics. One of the stars was Colette Bourgonje, a five-time Paralympian (cross-country sit-skier and wheelchair racer), who was a double bronze medallist.

Team sports, like ice hockey and soccer, have seen a remarkable growth in participation and success over the past couple of decades. More than 69,000 females were registered to play organized hockey in Canada in 2006 compared to less than 6,000 in the mid-1980s. The national team has enjoyed incredible success on the international stage: nine world titles in ten tries and Olympic titles in 2002 and 2006. Hayley Wickenheiser is the best female hockey player in the world; Cassie Campbell, now retired, is the first woman to do colour commentary on a *Hockey Night in Canada* broadcast and the first

Left: Now retired, Cassie Campbell was the first female hockey player to be elected to Canada's Sports Hall of Fame. Right: Christine Sinclair (number 12) is one of Canada's top soccer players.

female hockey player to be elected to Canada's Sports Hall of Fame. In the more than one hundred years that Canadian women have played the game, there have never been the same numbers, resources, programs, administrative structures and media focus as there are today.

Far more Canadian girls play soccer than do hockey, and the growth continues to be steady. Soccer has a much later history than hockey because it was not until the late 1960s, with the establishment of teams, leagues and school programs, that interest in youth soccer exploded. Of the total player registration in 2006, the number of females was 365,680, representing 43 percent. Although the vast majority of players are youths (under eighteen years), there are over 50,000 adult women in Canada playing the game. In 2007, the Canadian women's senior team was ranked ninth best in the world, and they have qualified for the 2008 Summer Olympics.

Canada is a world leader when it comes to the growth and influence of women's sport advocacy organizations. The Canadian Association for the Advancement of Women and Sport and Physical Activity (better known as CAAWS), founded in 1981, ensures that girls and women have access to a complete range of opportunities and choices and have equity as participants and leaders in sport and physical activity. It does this through building national partnerships with recreation and active living communities, Aboriginal sport groups, other multi-sport organizations and the women's health community; educating sport leaders and organizations about gender equity; maintaining a well-designed and interesting web site with loads of useful resource materials; and contributing to the international women's sport movement by sending representatives to conferences and working collaboratively with worldwide organizations. A number of advocacy organizations at the provincial level, such as proMOTION Plus in British Columbia, InMotion Network in Alberta and Égale Action in Quebec, sponsor a variety of programs aimed at getting more girls and women participating in sport and physical activity.

Many sport governing bodies now make a deliberate effort to encourage their members to develop gender equity statements and plans. Canadian Interuniversity Sport, for example, the organization that regulates and administers sport in Canadian universities, encourages university athletic departments to develop detailed plans to achieve gender equity and provides special funds to enhance women's programs. Beginning in the 1990s, there was a subtle shift in the discourse of human rights in Canada and elsewhere from "equality" to "equity." Equality generally meant "equality of opportunity" and women (along with other disadvantaged groups) were identified as target groups. In sport, equal opportunity programs were designed to increase women's overall participation by opening up opportunities for them to enjoy equal access. The shift to equity signalled a more comprehensive view where the focus was no longer exclusively on women (or any other group) but on a system, in this case sport, which needed to change to accommodate them.

On the negative side, boys are still more likely to participate in sport than are girls, although the gender gap is most noticeable in the five- to twelve-year-old range. Since the vast majority of sport participants do so in a competitive and structured environment, it means either that girls are not as keen as boys or there are still fewer

Danielle Peers (in red) is a Paralympic bronze medallist, world champion and world MVP in wheelchair basketball.

opportunities for girls than there are for boys. Despite the proliferation of advocacy programs to encourage more girls to become actively involved in sport and physical activity, the message often does not get through.

Diversity is also an ongoing issue. Aboriginal girls and women are often severely disadvantaged and marginalized, a problem recognized by both CAAWS and the Aboriginal Sport Circle, who have initiated a national project to increase community sport participation opportunities for Aboriginal girls and young women. Visible minority females, many of whom are immigrants, are greatly under-represented, especially

The Retreads basketball team in 2005, with an average age of 72.

in organized sport, where language, familiarity and cost can be significant barriers. Culture and sport sometimes clash, as witnessed recently in sports like soccer, judo and taekwondo, where Muslim youth wearing a hijab (head scarf) have been prevented from competing, ostensibly for safety reasons. For some, the hijab represents a symbol of their faith, and asking them to remove it violates their right to religious expression. Muslim sportswomen around the world wear the hijab when competing in a variety of sports, so it is strange for it to be an issue in Canada.

Athletes with disabilities, even those who perform spectacularly at the international level, such as the Paralympics, do not receive the same acclaim either in the media or popular consciousness as do able-bodied athletes. It is only in the 1990s that major international competitions, such as the Olympics and the Commonwealth Games, have seen the inclusion of selected full-medal events for disabled athletes. Elite sportswomen with disabilities should be constructed less as *disabled* sportswomen and more frequently as *sporting* heroines.

As the Canadian population ages, physical inactivity levels for adults over fifty-five is a concern, particularly for women because they tend to live longer than men. Inactive people are more susceptible to health problems such as increased obesity, high blood pressure and heart disease. Organizations like CAAWS have initiated projects aimed at increasing physical activity and sport opportunities for older women. Still, we don't hear enough about women who have been active all their lives and are still playing and competing.

At the World Master's Games in Edmonton in 2005, a Vancouver women's basketball team with an average age of seventy-two competed against younger, stronger and faster teams — some games they won, some they lost. Since they were the only team in their age category, they won the gold medal. The "Retreads," whose members were once some of the best women basketball players in Canada, are still active today. Darlene Currie, for example, was a member of three Pan-Am Games teams in the fifties and sixties, and went on to coach the women's national team; Mary MacDonald, who started her career at the University of Toronto in the early fifties, was also an all-star member of several Pan-Am teams. Some of these women have been playing basketball together for over fifty years.

The Canadian amateur sport system, from the local club right up to the national sport organizations, requires volunteers to help run it. Estimates show that 1.2 million Canadians (about 1 in 20) volunteer in sport as coaches, officials, leaders, administrators, board members and so forth. In Canadian society generally, women tend to volunteer more than men, but this is not the case in sport. Just over a third of sport volunteers are women; just over a quarter of volunteer coaches are women and nearly 40 percent of sport executives are women. Quite simply, women are under-represented in Canadian sport leadership — this is not an especially Canadian problem because it occurs worldwide. There is an ongoing attempt to do something about it through research studies and reports, special programs to encourage more women to become involved, and recognizing talented and devoted female sport leaders.

The lack of women coaches, especially at the higher levels, is also a problem receiving considerable attention. Women represent only 14.7 percent of Canada's Olympic coaches, whereas in university sport, national and provincial sport organizations, Canada Summer Games and other organizations women hold just over one third of the head and assistant coach positions. While gender equity has mostly been achieved when it comes to Canada's high-performance athletes, it has a long way to go for women in coaching.

Melody Davidson is head coach of Canada's national women's ice hockey team and Cornell University's Division I team.

The culture of sport promotes an idealized form of masculinity associated with toughness, power, aggressiveness, competitiveness and domination over others. Women coaches often demonstrate different leadership styles than men (more empathy, communication and co-operation) and have trouble fitting into this masculine culture. The sports culture is not very "family friendly" in that most athletes train before or after school and on weekends, making it difficult for women coaches with children to accommodate family responsibilities. Amateur sport lacks the resources necessary to develop and sustain support services such as job sharing and the provision of child care. Unlike other sectors of employment, sport has fallen behind in terms of gender equity, pay equity and affirmative action policies.

Nonetheless, there are increased opportunities for women to make a living playing sport aside from tennis and golf. Advertisers eager to find a way to connect with female consumers, television and Internet producers in need of programming, and a growing pool of professional calibre athletes, all explain the recent boom in women's professional team sports in North America. A few Canadian players have been drafted into the professional Women's National

Yoga classes are very popular, especially among women.

Basketball Association (WNBA), launched in 1997 by the NBA, with fourteen teams in two conferences. Before the WNBA, as is still the case now, several top Canadian players went to Europe to play professional or semi-professional basketball. Bev Smith, for example, undoubtedly the finest female player Canada has ever produced and former head coach of Canada's national women's team, played and coached in the Italian league for fourteen years.

Several Canadians also played in the Women's United Soccer Association, an eight-team professional league in the United States, which lasted from 2001 until 2003. With poor attendance and low television ratings, it could not survive, although there are plans afoot to launch another North American professional soccer league for women in 2009. Canada's top-level female ice hockey players hope one day to have a women's professional hockey league affiliated with the NHL, as the WNBA is with the NBA. Another positive development, certainly connected, is the new marketing of women's sport, especially team sports, which have gained unquestioned respect, and their women stars unprecedented celebrity.

Finally, statistics about fitness levels and inactivity among Canadian girls and women, and the gender inequities still present in the coaching and leadership ranks do not tell the whole story. Every day thousands of girls and women, from the very young to older seniors, can be found engaging in some sort of physical activity, whether climbing in playgrounds, jogging in the streets, riding bicycles, or purposively walking through shopping malls. Yoga classes are especially popular with women, and attract a huge variety of individuals, from the more spiritually inclined to those wishing to maintain their flexibility. Women's fitness classes, especially if they are inexpensive, easy to get to and have built-in child care, are popular and well attended. In winter, the mountain ski hills buzz with women of all ages who are fortunate enough to afford an expensive sport. The same is true of golf courses in summer, where opportunities for fun, companionship, competition and networking are drawing more females to learn the game. For the superbly fit, there are the many marathons and triathlons; more and more women enjoy "extreme" sports like rock climbing, parachute jumping, body boarding, mountain biking and others, for the same reasons — adventure, thrill, testing themselves — as do men.

EPILOGUE

In 1999, along with other end-of-millennium events, over 500 Canadian newspaper and broadcast outlets were asked to vote on the top ten Canadian male and female athletes and teams of the century. Among the latter, heavily weighted with men's professional sport teams, only one women's team made it — Sandra Schmirler's curling rink from 1993 to 1998. The Olympic gold medal winner and three-time world champion from Saskatchewan died tragically of cancer at age thirty-six in 2000. Further down the list in eleventh position was the Edmonton Grads basketball team, and in fifteenth place, the 1928 Olympic women's "Matchless Six" track team. Skier Nancy Greene was voted the century's top female athlete, followed by rower Silken Laumann, figure skater Barbara Ann Scott, biathlete Myriam Bédard, rower Marnie McBean, all-round athlete Bobbie Rosenfeld, speed skater Catriona Le May Doan, golfer Sandra Post, and swimmers Marilyn Bell and Elaine Tanner.

A panel at the *National Post* ranked the twenty-five most memorable moments in Canadian sports since 1948, only three of which related to women: Barbara Ann Scott's 1948 Olympic win, Nancy Greene's Olympic victories in 1968 and Silken Laumann's return from a devastating leg injury to win an Olympic bronze medal in 1992 at Barcelona. Observant readers pointed out that one glaring omission (among many) was Marilyn Bell's swim of Lake Ontario in 1954. TSN broadcast a six-part retrospective entitled "100 Years of Canadian Sports," which included a program about "innovators, movers, and shakers," a

Four-time Olympian Abby Hoffman became an outspoken voice for the plight of amateur athletes in Canada, especially women.

Atina Frod, Marcia Gudereit, Joan McCusker, Jan Betker and Sandra Schmirler celebrating their gold medal at the 1998 Nagano Winter Olympics.

tribute to the people who helped build and shape Canada's sport legacy. Not a single woman was mentioned.

Canada's sports halls of fame, which play a strategic role in the public remembering and

The "Matchless Six" at the 1928 Olympics: (left to right) chaperone Marie Parkes, Bobbie Rosenfeld, Jean Thompson, Ethel Smith, Myrtle Cook, Ethel Catherwood and Jane Bell.

Rower Silken Laumann overcame a devastating leg injury to win a bronze medal in the 1992 Barcelona Olympics.

interpretation of sports, have a dearth of women athletes and builders. Among the 489 recognized (as of 2007) in Canada's Sports Hall of Fame, only 71 (15 percent) are women, and in the Canadian Olympic Hall of Fame there are 104 (27 percent) women out of 380. A similar pattern exists in the thirty or so formal sports halls of fame and museums across the country. There is also an inexcusable lack of recognition of the contributions by female athletes of colour, Aboriginal women and athletes with disabilities among these awards and honours.

Women's sporting accomplishments are constantly compared to those of men, and male performance is the yardstick for *all* sport, including women's. This is wrong. One reason for these never-ending comparisons and the female athlete's marginalization is the persistent under-representation of women in sports journalism. The top daily newspapers in Canada rarely employ women sportswriters; the average space devoted to women's sport is less than 10 percent. In television sport, increasingly more women appear in front of the cameras, a few more behind; yet women's sport in Canada, except for curling, figure skating and the Olympics every two years, is noticeably absent from the major networks — although it is more prevalent on specialty cable channels and everywhere in the new media, such as the Internet.

Most importantly, to place too much emphasis on a small group of highly talented athletes, either female or male, is to diminish the accomplishments of the thousands of other athletes, some of whom make it to the podium, but most of whom do not. It also neglects the role played by parents, siblings, teachers, coaches, spouses, friends and others, many of whom are women, who support and encourage these athletes, sometimes at considerable personal sacrifice over many years. We need to recognize them all.

NOTABLE FIRSTS AND ACHIEVEMENTS IN CANADIAN WOMEN'S SPORT

1858 — Montreal Ladies Archery Club, the earliest known sports club for women in Canada, is formed

1861 — Ladies' Prince of Wales Club of Montreal, a snowshoeing club, is founded

1882 — Louise Armaindo, from Ste-Clet near Montreal, becomes famous as "the female champion bicycle rider of the world"

1883 — Maude Delano-Osborne wins the first Canadian Ladies tennis championship

1891 — first press account of a women's ice hockey game between two teams in Ottawa

1894 — Royal Montreal Curling Club organizes the Ladies' Auxiliary Club, the first women's curling club in the world

1896 — National Council of Women praises the bicycle for its role in dress reform and encouraging exercise among women

1901 — first Canadian Ladies' Amateur Golf Championship is held in Toronto, won by Lilly Young of the Royal Montreal Golf Club

1902 — challenge ice hockey match between clubs in Trois-Rivières and Montreal is considered the first championship of Canada

1905 — first Canadian women's figure skating title is won by Anne Ewan of the Earl Grey Skating Club in Montreal

1906 — Lois Moyes Bickle wins the first of ten Canadian singles tennis championships and later eight doubles championships (with Florence Best)

1913 — Florence Harvey becomes the first organizing secretary of the Canadian Ladies' Golf Union and the first women's sport executive

1921 — Gladys Robinson competes in the world speed skating championship at Lake Placid, New York, winning all her events
— Toronto Ladies Athletic Club, the first all-women's multi-sport club in Canada, is founded

1922 — Edmonton Grads win the first Canadian women's basketball championship
— Ladies Ontario Hockey Association, the first provincial association, is formed

1924 — Cecil Eustace Smith competes in figure skating at the Winter Olympics in Chamonix, France, becoming the first Canadian woman Olympian
— Edmonton Grads win the first women's world title in basketball in France (they will go on to compile a record of 502 wins and only 20 losses, disbanding in 1940)
— Phyllis Munday becomes the first woman to climb Mount Robson, the highest peak in the Canadian Rockies
— Ada MacKenzie, Canada's outstanding female golfer, opens the Toronto Ladies' Golf and Tennis Club in Thornhill, Ontario

1926 — Women's Amateur Athletic Federation of Canada is formed, with over 1,200 registered athletes (it amalgamates with the men's Amateur Athletic Union of Canada in 1954)
— Lela Brooks breaks six world speed skating records and wins the world championship
— First Canadian synchronized swimming championship is held in Montreal

1928 — Alexandrine Gibb, the first Canadian woman sportswriter, begins writing her "No Man's Land of Sport" column for the Toronto Daily Star
— "Matchless Six" (Florence Bell, Ethel Catherwood, Myrtle Cook, Fanny "Bobbie" Rosenfeld, Ethel Smith and Jean Thompson) win two gold medals, a silver and bronze at the Amsterdam Olympics
— Dorothy Prior is the first Canadian woman to compete in Olympic swimming events

1930 — Cecil Eustace Smith is the first Canadian to win a world figure skating championship medal (she comes second to Sonja Henie)

1932 — Preston Rivulettes begin their domination of Canadian women's ice hockey, eventually winning 350 games, tying three and losing only two (they disband in 1941)

1934 — swimmer Phyllis Dewar wins four gold medals at the British Empire Games in London, England

1935 — Seigniory Ski Club in Montebello, Quebec, institutes the first Canadian downhill skiing championships for women

1938 — Barbara Howard, the first Canadian woman of colour to compete internationally, competes for Canada at the British Empire Games in Sydney, Australia

1939 — Dorothy Walton captures the All-England title, badminton's equivalent of the world amateur championship

1943 — 64 of over 600 women who played in the All-American Girls Professional Baseball League were Canadian (the league closes in 1954)

1947 — Barbara Ann Scott is the first Canadian to win a world figure skating championship

1948 — Barbara Ann Scott wins the first Canadian Olympic gold medal in figure skating
— Shirley Gordon, a disabled high-jumper, competes for Canada at the Summer Olympics

1950 — Rosella Thorne is the only Black woman athlete named to the Canadian British Empire Games team (and the 1952 Summer Olympic team and the 1954 British Empire and Commonwealth Games team)
— Bobbie Rosenfeld, all-round athlete, coach and sportswriter, is named top female athlete of the half-century in Canada

1951 — Winnie Roach Leuszler is the first Canadian to swim the English Channel

— Marlene Stewart (later Streit and still competing) begins her golf career by defeating veteran Ada MacKenzie at the Ontario ladies' golf championship

1954 — Marilyn Bell becomes the first person to swim across Lake Ontario

— skaters Frances Dafoe (with Norris Bowden) are the first Canadians to be World Pairs champions

1956 — Lucile Wheeler is the first Canadian to win a skiing medal at the Olympics

— Abby ("Ab") Hoffman, a nine-year-old defence stalwart for the St. Catharines Tee Pees, is barred from playing hockey in a boys' league (she went on to become a four-time Olympic runner)

— Irene MacDonald wins Canada's first Olympic diving medal, a bronze

1960 — Elaine McCrossan is the first Canadian woman to achieve a black belt in judo

1963 — ringette is invented by Sam Jacks in North Bay as an alternative to women's hockey

1966 — swimmer Elaine Tanner wins six medals at the British Empire and Commonwealth Games, contributing to the best Canadian team showing since 1934

1967 — first official Canadian women's ice hockey championship is held in Brampton, Ontario

— Nancy Greene is the women's Overall World Cup skiing champion (she repeats this in 1968)

1968 — Sandra Post, the first Canadian woman to play on the LPGA tour, defeats the number one American player

— Phyllis Bomberry is the first female recipient of the Tom Longboat Award, given annually to the most outstanding Aboriginal athlete

1969 — Dorothy Lidstone becomes the first Canadian world champion in archery

1971 — Debbie Brill, a Canadian, is the first woman in North America to high-jump six feet

1972 — Roseanne Allen and Sharon and Shirley Firth, cross-country skiers, are the first Canadian Aboriginal women to compete in an Olympic Games

— Jocelyne Bourassa becomes the second Canadian to play with the LGPA

1974 — first National Conference on Women and Sport, held in Toronto

1976 — Sue Holloway is the only Canadian woman to have competed in two Olympics in the same year (cross-country skiing and kayaking)

1977 — Canadian marathon swimmer Cindy Nicholas becomes the first person to complete a double crossing of the English Channel

1979 — Pat Messner is the first Canadian to win a world championship in waterskiing

1980 — the Female Athlete Conference, second national conference on women and sport, is held in Vancouver

— creation of the Women's Program within the federal government's Fitness and Amateur Sport Branch

— Bev Beaver, all-round athlete from the Six Nations reserve, wins the Tom Longboat Award

1981 — founding of the Canadian Association for the Advancement of Women and Sport and Physical Activity (CAAWS)

— Abby Hoffman is the first woman appointed director general of Sport Canada

1984 — Anne Ottenbrite is the first Canadian woman to win a gold medal in Olympic swimming

1986 — Sharon Wood, a Canadian, is the first North American woman to scale Mount Everest

— the Ontario Court of Appeal strikes down a discriminatory clause in the Ontario Human Rights Code preventing girls from playing on all-male sports teams

1987 — Betty Baxter founds the National Coaching School for Women, a women-centred and athlete-centred approach to coaching

1988 — Justine Blainey finally wins the right to play in the all-male Ontario Hockey Association

— Carol Anne Letheren is the first woman to be chef de mission of a Canadian Olympic team

1988 — marathon swimmer Vicky Keith is the first person to swim across all five of the Great Lakes

1990 — Carol Anne Letheren is the first woman elected president of the Canadian Olympic Association, becoming the first Canadian woman to sit on the International Olympic Committee

1992 — Colette Bourgonje, a cross-country sit-skier and wheelchair racer, competes in her first Winter Paralympics (she goes on to compete in eight Summer and Winter Paralympic Games)

— rower Silken Laumann returns from a devastating injury to win an Olympic bronze medal

1994 — biathlete Myriam Bédard is the first Canadian to win two Winter Olympic gold medals

— Judy Kent is Canada's first female chef de mission at the Commonwealth Games

1996 — Charmaine Crooks, a five-time Olympian, is the first Canadian woman of colour, and only the second Canadian woman, to sit on the International Olympic Committee

1997 — kayaker Caroline Brunet becomes the first woman to win three gold medals at a world championship

1999 — skier Nancy Greene is named the century's top female athlete in Canada

2002 — Clara Hughes wins an Olympic bronze in speed skating, becoming the first Canadian to win medals in both the Summer and Winter Olympics (she had won two bronze cycling medals in 1996)

2004 — at the Athens Olympics, 50 percent of Canada's medals and 53 percent of the nation's top-eight finishes were earned by female athletes

2006 — speed skater Cindy Klassen wins five medals at the Winter Olympics

— Olympian Beckie Scott is elected to the International Olympic Committee

— Cassie Campbell, former captain of the Canadian Women's Hockey Team, is the first woman doing colour commentary on *Hockey Night in Canada*

2007 — Cassie Campbell is the first female hockey player elected to Canada's Sports Hall of Fame

WHERE TO FIND MORE INFORMATION ABOUT CANADA'S ATHLETIC HEROINES

Alberta Sports Hall of Fame and Museum

#30 Riverview Park, Red Deer, AB, T4N 1E3
www.albertasportshalloffame.com

Brief biographies, but no photos, are available in electronic form for all inductees.

British Columbia Sports Hall of Fame and Museum

Gate "A" — BC Place Stadium, 777 Pacific Boulevard South, Vancouver, BC, V6B 4Y8
www.bcsportshalloffame.com

This museum has an ongoing exhibit called *In Her Footsteps … Celebrating BC Women in Sport*, an annual recognition program honouring women who have made a significant contribution to sport and physical activity in British Columbia. Brief biographies and photos in electronic form are available for all inductees.

Canada's Sports Hall of Fame

115 Princes' Blvd, Exhibition Place, Toronto, ON, M6K 3C3
www.cshof.ca

Their website, in both English and French, contains an excellent virtual collection pertaining to the history of sport in Canada. It includes artifacts, archival photos, videos and in some cases interviews with its nearly 500 inductees (15 percent of whom are women).

Canadian Association for the Advancement of Women and Sport and Physical Activity

N202-801 King Edward Avenue,
Ottawa, ON, K1N 6N5
www.caaws.ca

CAAWS maintains an outstanding website with all sorts of useful information pertaining to girls and women in sports and physical activity.

Canadian Golf Hall of Fame and Museum

Glen Abbey Golf Club, 1333 Dorval Drive,
Oakville, ON, L6J 4Z3
www.rcga.org

Brief biographies and photos in electronic form are available for all inductees. Their heritage services include an extensive photographic and documentary archive as well as a golf library.

Canadian Olympic Hall of Fame

Contact: Canadian Olympic Committee
Suite 900, 21 St. Clair Avenue East, Toronto, ON, M4T 1L9
www.olympic.ca/EN/hof/index.shtml

It is not possible to obtain biographical profiles or photos of their inductees.

Canadian Ski Museum

The Canadian Ski Museum, 1960 Scott Street,
Ottawa, ON, K1Z 8L8
www.skimuseum.ca

This museum has an unparalleled collection of artifacts and archival holdings related to Canadian ski heritage, only a fraction of which are available through their website. Full biographies and several photos in electronic form are available for all inductees to its hall of fame.

Canadian Tennis Hall of Fame

Contact: Tennis Canada, Suite 100, 1 Shoreham Drive, Toronto, ON, M3N 3A6
www.tenniscanada.com/tennis_canada/Pub/HallOfFame.aspx

Although brief biographies and photos in electronic form are available for all inductees, the information is very sketchy for most.

Manitoba Sports Hall of Fame and Museum

5th floor — The Bay Downtown, 450 Portage Avenue, Winnipeg, MB, R3C 0E7
www.halloffame.mb.ca

Brief biographies and photos in electronic form are available for all inductees.

New Brunswick Sports Hall of Fame

John Thurston Clark Memorial Building
503 Queen Street, Fredericton, NB, E3B 1B8
www.nbsportshalloffame.nb.ca

Brief biographies (in both French and English) and photos are available in electronic form for all inductees.

Newfoundland and Labrador Sports Hall of Fame

Contact: Sport Newfoundland and Labrador
P.O. Box 8700, St. John's, NL, A1B 4J6
www.sportnl.ca/programs/hall_of_fame/index.html

Brief biographies and photos are available in electronic form for all inductees. See also the wonderful virtual exhibit "Women in Sport: Pre-Confederation Newfoundland," sponsored by the provincial archives: www.therooms.ca/archives/wis/

Nova Scotia Sport Hall of Fame

Location: Halifax Metro Centre
Contact: Suite 446, 1800 Argyle Street, Halifax, NS, B3J 3N8
www.novascotiasporthalloffame.com

Brief biographies and photos are available in electronic form for all inductees.

ONTARIO

The province of Ontario does not have a central sports hall of fame or museum, but throughout the province there are several local sports halls of fame, such as these:

Collingwood & District Sports Hall of Fame

No contact information provided.
www.collingwoodsportshalloffame.ca

Brief biographies and photos are available in electronic form for all inductees. One of the few sports halls of fame where inductees are categorized by gender.

Etobicoke Sports Hall of Fame

5110 Dundas Street West, Toronto, ON, M9A 1C2
www.etobicokesports.ca

Brief biographies and photos are available in electronic form for all inductees.

Glengarry Sports Hall of Fame

Location: Fair Grounds, Maxville
Contact: Box 282, Maxville, ON, K0C 1T0
www.glengarrysports.com

Well-written biographies and colour paintings are available in electronic form for all inductees.

Ottawa Sports Hall of Fame

Scotiabank Place
1000 Palladium Drive, Box 103, Kanata, ON, K2V 1A4
www.ottawasportshalloffame.com

Brief biographies and photos are available in electronic form for all inductees.

Northwestern Ontario Sports Hall of Fame

219 May Street South, Thunder Bay, ON, P7E 1B5

www.nwosportshalloffame.com

At the time of writing their website was under construction and it was not possible to obtain information pertaining to its inductees.

Prince Edward Island Sports Hall of Fame and Museum

Location: Wyatt Centre, Summerside
Contact: P.O. Box 1523, Summerside, PE, C1N 4K4
www.peisportshalloffame.ca

Brief biographies and photos are available in electronic form for all inductees.

Saskatchewan Sports Hall of Fame and Museum

2205 Victoria Avenue, Regina, SK, S4P 0S4
www.sshfm.com

Information pertaining to their inductees is not available in electronic form, although this museum provides research services for a fee. It is possible to obtain some information about their inductees, as well as other sporting heroines, from Saskatchewan, through a website maintained by the Saskatoon Public Library. See:
www.saskatoonlibrary.ca/sports/pages/welcome.html

Skate Canada Hall of Fame

Contact: Skate Canada
865 Shefford Road, Ottawa, ON, K1J 1H9
www.skatecanada.ca/en/about_skate_canada/hall_of_fame/honoured_members

Brief biographies and photos are available in electronic form for all inductees. The Skate Canada Archives contain photos, videotapes, artifacts and other materials, which are available for consultation by appointment with an archivist.

Sport Yukon Hall of Fame

Contact: 4061—4th Avenue, Whitehorse, YT, Y1A 1H1
www.sportyukon.com/hallOfFame/default.php

Brief biographies and photos are available in electronic form for all inductees.

Temple de la renommée du sport du Québec

Contact: 945, rue Dawson, Dorval, PQ, J4Z 3P5
www.rds.ca/pantheon/pantheon_bienvenue.html

Brief biographies (in French) and photos are available in electronic form for all inductees.

FURTHER READING

The story of women's sport in Canada is not well documented. My own book, *The Girl and the Game: A History of Women's Sport in Canada* (Broadview Press, 2002), is an attempt to provide a comprehensive history of women and sport in Canada, but as I point out at the end of this book, we need to fill in the missing details through regional and local stories as well as through studies of specific sports and biographies of our athletic heroines. This is beginning to happen as graduate students research their theses and dissertations, but little of this new material has yet been published.

Earlier, more specific, histories of women's sport in Canada include the following: Helen Lenskyj, *Out of Bounds: Women, Sport and Sexuality* (Women's Press, 1986); Brian McFarlane, *Proud Past, Bright Future: One Hundred Years of Canadian Women's Hockey* (Stoddart, 1994); and Elizabeth Etue and Megan Williams, *On the Edge: Women Making Hockey History* (Second Story Press, 1996). There are few published histories of specific sports and no provincial or territorial histories of women's sports in Canada. An exception is a small volume published through the Canadian Ladies' Professional Golf Association — Saskatchewan and the Saskatchewan Sports Hall of Fame and Museum by Sandra Bingaman, *Breaking 100: A Century of Women's Sport in Saskatchewan*. Especially helpful are club histories such as Tim O'Connor, *The Ladies' 1924–1999: A History of the Ladies' Golf Club of Toronto* (Dundurn Press, 1999).

We are only beginning to see well-researched biographies of Canadian women sports personalities. Two excellent volumes published recently are Byron Rempel, *No Limits: The Amazing Story of Rhona and Rhoda Wurtele* (Twinski Publications, 2007), and Sally Manning, *Guts and Glory: The Arctic Skiers Who Challenged the World* (Outcrop, The Northern Publishers, 2006), which is about Aboriginal Olympians, especially Sharon and Shirley Firth. Wendy Long's *Celebrating Excellence: Canadian Women Athletes* (Polestar, 1995) still remains very useful.

There are a few general histories of Canadian sport that contain chapters related to women. For example, Bruce Kidd, *The Struggle for Canadian Sport* (University of Toronto Press, 1996), has an excellent chapter on women's sport between the two world wars. Colin Howell, *Blood, Sweat, and Cheers: Sport and the Making of Modern Canada* (University of Toronto Press, 2001), has a chapter related to gender, as does Don Morrow and Kevin Wamsley's *Sport in Canada: A History* (Oxford University Press, 2005).

Finally, there is an increasing number of popular histories being published, which, although useful, are written for younger audiences. Among the most recent are Ron Hotchkiss, *The Matchless Six: The Story of Canada's First Woman's Olympic Team* (Tundra Books, 2006), and Anne Dublin, *Bobbie Rosenfeld: The Olympian Who Could Do Everything* (Second Story Press, 2004).

ACKNOWLEDGEMENTS

The historical study of sport in Canada is a growing field, and I owe an enormous debt to those who have contributed to our understanding of this rich sporting heritage. It includes academic papers and books as well as provincial, regional and local studies right down to the club level; it also includes a vast popular history about our sporting heroes. But we know much less about our athletic heroines.

I would also like to acknowledge the many students, colleagues, archivists and reference librarians who have assisted me in my research over the past four decades. At times I have personally visited local and provincial archives and museums as well as many of the growing number of sports halls of fame and museums, always to be met by enthusiastic and patient staff willing to share their knowledge and expertise.

Michael Harrison at Broadview Press graciously gave us permission to draw upon material from my previously published *The Girl and the Game: A History of Women's Sport in Canada*. Nancy Mitchell applied her fabulous genealogical sleuthing skills to help ferret out valuable biographical information. As always, the text has benefited from Jane Haslett's editorial skills.

Finally, I want to thank James Lorimer and Company for inviting me to undertake this project. A special thank you is owed to the editors and staff there, especially Lynn Schellenberg, who worked hard to acquire the best images and make the publication process go smoothly.

VISUAL CREDITS

Alpine Canada Alpin: 74; Archives of Ontario: 25; Blue Heron Media Ltd.: 84TL; British Columbia Sports Hall of Fame: 22, 42, 44, 58, 78; Canada Science and Technology Museum: 15, 18; Canada's Sports Hall of Fame: 31, 35, 37BR, 40T, 40B, 45, 50, 51, 54TL, 60R, 61, 62, 64L, 65, 66T, 66M, 73, 87T; *Canadian Magazine*, August 29, 1970, p. 6: 72; Canadian Museum of Civilization: 10, 13T, 28BL, 52B; Canadian Olympian Collection, Library and Archives Canada: 75, 76, 77, 80, 82R, 87B, 88B; Canadian War Museum: 55; Canadian Wheelchair Basketball Association: 83; City of Cambridge Archives Photograph Collection: 47; City of Edmonton Archives: 60L, 67; City of Toronto Archives: 20, 21, 28TR, 30, 36, 41T, 41B; Commemorative AAGPBL cards produced by Larry Fritsch Cards, available through www.fritschcards.com: 57; Courtesy of Phyllis Bomberry: 69R; Courtesy of Winnie Roach Leuszler: 64R; Courtesy of Jackie MacDonald: 56; Courtesy of Bill McNulty: 49; Courtesy of Rosella Thorne: 68; David Young, *The Golden Age of Canadian Figure Skating*: 33; Glenbow Museum: 29; Henry Roxborough, *One Hundred Not Out*: 8TR; Hockey Canada: 81, 82L, 85; iStock Photo: No copyright holder: 70BM, 86; Duncan Babbage: 77BR; Julie Masson Dehaies: 69BM; Bonnie Jacobs: 79; William Mahar: Contents page; Nick Schlax: 84BR; Ladies Golf Club of Toronto: 34; Library and Archives Canada: 7, 9, 11, 13B, 37T, 38, 52T, 88T; McCord Museum: 6, 8L, 14, 26, 27, 28TL; *The National Police Gazette*, May 10, 1884, p.6: 12; New Brunswick Sports Hall of Fame: 19, 23R; Nova Scotia Archives and Records Management: 17; NWT Archives: 70T; Personal collection of M. Ann Hall: 48; Photo by Frank Grant, originally appeared on cover of *Maclean's*, September 17, 1966 edition: 71; Provincial Archives of Alberta: 32; Royal Canadian Golf Association: 23L, 59; The Rooms Provincial Archives, Sports Archives of Newfoundland and Labrador collection: 24; Skate Canada Archives: 53L, 53R; Toronto Port Authority Archives: 39; Toronto Public Library Digital Collections: 16; *The Toronto Star*: 43, 63; *True Comics*, No. 35, May 1944: 54M; Woodland Cultural Centre, Brantford ON: 46.

INDEX

Aboriginal athletes and sports, 10–11, 46, 69, 70, 82–83
administration and leadership, 22–23, 34–35, 42–43, 45, 82–85
Aitkins, Roxy, 43
Alberta, 24, 30, 47, 60, 83
Allen, Roseanne, 70
Anderson, Jessie, 9
Armaindo, Louise (Brisbois), 12–13

Babbitt, Ethel (Hatt), 19, 21
baby boom, 55
badminton, 19, 21, 46, 54–55, 70, 78
Baker, Mary "Bonnie," 57
Banff Winter Carnival (1906), 30
Barber, Sara, 65
Barclay, James, 78
baseball, 19, 40, 57, 68, 78; See also softball
basketball: age of players in, 84; championships, 58, 83; in education system, 25–26, 28–29; opportunities in, 85–86; rule variations, 31, 39, 47–48; run by women, 35; Underwood Trophy, 31
Beaton, Mary, 28
Beaver, Bev, 69
Bédard, Myriam, 87
Beers, George, 10
Bell, Jane, 36, 38, 88
Bell, Margaret, 49
Bell, Marilyn, 60–63, 87
Berto, Stephanie, 77
Best, Florence, 21
Betker, Jan, 87
Bickle, Lois Moyes, 21
Blanker-Koen, Fanny "Flying Dutchwoman," 67
Bloomer, Amelia, 14
bloomers, 14, 18, 28, 31, 35; See also sportswear
Bobbie Rosenfeld trophy, 59; See also Rosenfeld, Fanny "Bobbie"
Bomberry, Phyllis "Yogi," 69
Bourassa, Jocelyne, 77–78
Bourgonje, Colette, 81
bowling, 21, 46
Boys, Bev, 78
Brill, Debbie, 76–77
British Columbia, 22, 30, 42, 47, 49, 65, 73, 83
British Empire and Commonwealth Games, 56, 68, 73
British Empire Games, 48, 49, 68
Brooks, Lela (Potter), 40–41, 48

CAAWS, 82–83, 84
Caledonia Indians (softball, Six Nations), 46
Callow, Eleanor "Squirt," 57
Callwood, June, 56–57
Campbell, Cassie, 81–82
Campbell, Frances, 23
Canada Games (1969), 69
Canadian Belles (football), 71–72
Canadian Ladies Athletic Club, 35

Canadian Ladies' Golf Union (CLGU), 23, 50
Canadian Ladies' Professional Golf Association, 78
Canadian National Exhibition (CNE), 35, 38, 41–42, 58, 61–62, 65
Canadian Women's Army Corps, 55
Cartwright, Ethel Mary, 26–27
Catherwood, Ethel, 36–38, 76, 88
Chadwick, Florence, 61–62
Chicago Down Drafts (softball), 47
Chicago Flyers (track and field), 35
Clark, C.S., 17
class: athletes from privilege, 65; cost of skating, 25; ice hockey, 39; marathon swimming, 63; sport and the middle class, 19–20, 27; sport as affordable, 43–44; support for the working class, 34–35, 45–46
Cleary, Nora, 25–26
Cleveland Erin Brews (softball), 47
climbing, 19, 86
Cochu, Francine, 72
Coleridge, Francis G., 7
Commonwealth Games, 70, 84
Comstock Racing Team, 71
Conacher, Grace, 35
Cook, Myrtle (McGowan), 35–38, 39, 44, 48, 58, 74, 79, 88
Crawford, Judy, 78
cricket, 19, 46
Cumming, George, 34
curling, 23–24, 87
Currie, Darlene, 84
cycling, 12–16, 18

Darling, Judy (Evans), 59
Davidson, Melody, 85
Dawes, Eva, 48
Delano-Osborne, Maude, 20, 33–34
Depression, 46, 48
Detroit Rainbows (softball), 47
Dewar, Phyllis, 48
Didrikson, Mildred "Babe," 48
diversity, 83–84, 88; See also Aboriginal athletes and sports; race diving, 64
Dominion ladies' championship (tennis, Rogers Cup), 20
Dominion ladies' golf championship, 22
Dominion women's championship (basketball), 31

Earl Grey Skating Club (Montreal), 25
Edmonton, 24, 28–29, 50, 84
Edmonton Graduates (Grads) (basketball), 29, 31, 39, 44–45, 47, 49–50, 87
Edmonton Mortons (softball), 58
Edmonton Rustlers (ice hockey), 47
educational system, 18, 25–27, 34, 44–45, 79, 83
Edwards, Miss (of New York), 9–10
Eisler, Brenda, 77
Ewan, Anne, 25

Fédération sportive féminine internationale (FSFI), 35
"Feminine Sports Reel" (Rosenfeld), 39
Ferguson, Elmer, 43
Firth, Sharon and Shirley, 70
Fisher, Lenore, 65
fitness classes, 86
Fizzell, Mildred, 48
Frayne, Trent, 59
Fredericton Golf Club, 21
Frizzel, Mary, 48
Frod, Atina, 87

Garapick, Nancy, 74–75
gender boundaries, 70–71, 79–81, 82–83, 85, 88; after the war, 55; clothing, 14–15; in cycling, 16, 18; sports modified for women, 11, 12; See also morality and deportment
Gibb, Alexandrine, 34–36, 39, 43–46, 49–50, 61–62, 79
"Girl and the Game, The" (Griffiths), 39
golf: as acceptable, 19; championships, 22–23, 59, 61; competition, 20; cost of memberships, 34; fundraising through, 50; "Ladies" clubs, 21–22; LPGA Tour, 77–78; number of clubs, 22; run by women, 34; on television, 77
Gorman, Charlie, 33
government, 17, 73
Grads. See Edmonton Graduates (Grads) (basketball)
Granite rink (Toronto), 15, 52
Granites (ice hockey), 33
Grant, Virginia, 65
grass hockey, 19
Greene, Nancy, 73, 74, 77, 87
Grey, Lady Evelyn (Evelyn Jones), 25
Grey, Lord, 25
Griffin, Audrey, 41–42
Griffin, Frederick, 44
Griffiths, Phyllis, 39, 46, 79
Grosse, Rosa (O'Neill), 35, 44
Gudereit, Marcia, 87
gymnastics, 26

H.A. Lozier & Co. (Toronto), 15
Halifax, 14, 22, 26–27, 36, 74
Hall, Lucy, 16
Hamilton Golf Club, 22
Hart House, 71
Harvey, Florence, 22–23
Harvey, Gail (Moore), 59
Haycock, Aimee, 25
Hedin, Edith, 42
Heggtveit, Anne, 66
Henie, Sonja, 33–34, 52–53
Hewson, Joanne, 65
Hinde and Dauch softball, 35
Hitchens, Gayle (Borthwick), 59
Hoffman, Abby, 71, 74, 78, 79, 87
Holland, Nancy and Janet, 66

horsemanship, 8, 11, 19, 51
Howard, Barbara, 49
Hyde, Ernest, 28–29
Hyslop school (Toronto), 15

Ice Capades and Follies, 52–53
ice hockey: championships, 30, 47, 81; coaching, 85; early history of, 29–30; popularity of, 39–40, 47, 58, 79; professional league, 86
Indian-club swinging, 26–27
International Amateur Athletic Federation, 36
International Skating Union, 40
"In the Women's Sportlight" (Cook), 39

Jenkins, Dorothy, 33
Jeux olympiques féminins (Paris), 35–36
Johnson, Dorothy and Daisy, 31, 32
Jones, Diane, 77
judo, 70, 84

Kilberry, Miss (of Boston), 9
Klassen, Cindy, 81
Knickerbocker Club (Toronto), 13
Kruger, Carlyn, 65–66

lacrosse, 10–11, 19
Ladies Ontario Hockey Association, 39–40
Ladies' Prince of Wales Club of Montreal, 7
Lakeshore Swimming Club (Toronto), 61–62
Langlais, Monique, 65
Langley's Lakesides (softball), 47
lawn tennis, 19
Laumann, Silken, 87–88
Le May Doan, Catriona, 87
Lennox, Diana Gordon, 49
Little, Olive "Ollie" (Bend), 57
Lou Marsh Trophy, 59, 61
Loverock, Patty, 77
Lytle, Andy, 43

MacDonald, Irene, 64
MacDonald, Jackie, 56–57
MacDonald, Mary, 84
MacDonald, Noel, 45
MacKenzie, Ada, 34, 59
Madison Square Garden, 12, 34, 47
Magnussen, Karen, 78
Manitoba, 47, 58; See also Winnipeg
Martin, Andrée, 78
Martin, Winnie, 31, 32
Masterman, W.K., 14
McBean, Marnie, 87
McCarthy, Norah, 52
McCarthy, Tasie, 52
McCreath, Ralph, 52
McCrossan, Elaine, 70–71
McCusker, Joan, 87
McDougall High School (Edmonton), 28–29
McGill School of Physical Education, 26–27

McInnes, Gordon, 61
McKenzie, Violet, 68
McKinley, Nancy, 78
McLeod Ryan, Doreen, 67
media: on acceptable sports, 7, 19; athletes as daughters or children, 59, 60, 62–63, 65, 74–75; athletes sexualized, 74–77; on basketball, 31–32; bloomers, 14; colour commentary, 81; criticism of, 79; on cycling, 15–16; on femininity, 43–45, 55–56, 75–76, 78; on ice hockey, 30; lack of coverage, 69–70, 72; on "lady cyclist," 13; on losing, 75; for Marilyn Bell, 62; on marital status of athletes, 44; on Native women, 11; for 1924 Olympics, 33; recognition of athletes, 59, 68, 78, 87–88; respect for athletes, 32–33; on skating, 40, 51–52; sports as glamorous, 53–55; on swearing, 22; Victorian era, 10; women's names in, 20; See also morality and deportment; sportswriters
medical professionals: ; on competing mothers, 60, 63, 67; on cycling, 15–16; on reproductive health, 44; in Victorian era, 10
Milliat, Alice, 35
Minto Skating Club (Ottawa), 24–25, 33, 51
Mitchell, Elizabeth, 16
Monaghan, Anne, 66
Montreal: curling, 23–24; cycling, 14; football, 72; golf, 21–22; Olympics, 38, 75, 79; skating, 25; sports run by women, 34–35; tobogganing, 9; in Victorian era, 7; Victoria Rink, 6; See also Quebec
Montreal clubs, 7, 21–24, 25, 68
Morahan, Jessie, 9–10
morality and deportment: acceptable sports, 19, 44–45, 53–54; after the war, 55–56; in basketball, 31–32; in golf, 22; 1950s athlete image, 60; and women cyclists, 17–18; See also gender boundaries; media
Mountifield, Eleanor, 31, 32
Muslim sportswomen, 84

National Council of Women of Canada, 16
Nesukaitis, Violetta, 78
New Brunswick, 21, 22–23, 41, 47
Newfoundland, 13, 24
New Woman, 18, 20, 27
"No Man's Land of Sport" (Gibb), 39
Northwest Territories, 70
Nova Scotia, 17, 22, 47; See also Halifax

Of Toronto the Good (Clark, 1898), 17
Ohsweken Mohawk Ladies (softball), 69
Oke, Fred G. "Teddy," 37, 41
Olympic Games: as acceptable for women, 45; Athens (2004), 80–81; Barcelona (1992), 87–88; costs, 48, 49; first women (1924), 33; Innsbruck (1964),

68; London (1948), 67; Mexico City; (1968), 74, 87; Montreal (1976), 75, 79; Nagano (1998), 87; Paralympics, 80–81, 84; Sapporo (1972), 78; and Second World War, 50, 52; Squaw Valley [1960], 66, 67–68; St. Moritz (1928), 34; St. Moritz (1948), 51, 55, 87; Summer (1928), 35–38, 87–88; Summer (1932), 48; Summer (1952), 68; Summer (2008), 82; Tokyo (1964), 76; Torino (2006), 81; Winter (1932), 48; Winter (1936), 48–49; Winter (1956), 65–66; Winter (1972), 70
O'Meara, Eleanor, 52
Ontario: basketball, 25–26, 47; bloomers, 14; curling, 24; cycling, 16; golf, 59, 77; ice hockey, 40; marathon swimming, 62; skating, 24–25; skiing, 70; softball, 46; sports in education, 45; in Victorian era, 7–8; See also Ottawa; Toronto
Ottawa, 7, 16, 20, 24–25, 29, 33, 51
Ouellette, Caroline, 81

Pacific Northwest championship (golf), 22
Page, J. Percy, 28–29, 31, 32, 44, 47
Palmer, Lillian, 48
Pan-American Games, 56, 65, 70, 84
Parkdale clubs (Toronto), 37
Parkes, Marie, 36, 88
pedestrianism/walking, 8–10, 19
Peers, Danielle, 83
Percival, Lloyd, 56
Perry, Nellie, 31
Peticlerc, Chantal, 80
Pitt, Faye, 66
Post, Sandra, 34, 77, 78, 87
Preston Rivulettes (ice hockey, Ontario), 47
Prior, Dorothy, 36–37
prize money, 12, 41–42, 51, 61–64, 78–79
professionalism, 52–53, 56, 61

Quebec: advocacy for gender equity, 83; basketball, 47; curling, 24; cycling, 13; golf, 78; ice hockey, 29–30; skating, 24; skiing, 65; in Victorian era, 8; See also Montreal

race, 49, 68; See also Aboriginal athletes and sports
Raine, Al, 73
Reiser, Glenda, 78
Retreads basketball team, 84
Rideau Skating Club, 24
Ritchie, Grace, 16
Roach Leuszler, Winnie, 63–65
Robinson, Gladys, 40
Robinson, Jackie, 68
Robson, Fred, 40
Rogers, Melville, 33
roller skating, 7, 9, 25, 71
Rosenfeld, Fanny "Bobbie," 35–36, 38–39, 43, 45, 55, 74, 79, 87–88
rounders, 19
rowing/water regattas, 7, 11, 19, 87–88
rugby, 19

Ruys de Perez, Stephanie, 71
Ryder, Gus, 60–61

safety, 15, 46, 87–88
Samuel, Constance (Wilson), 52
Sander, Helen, 70
Saskatchewan, 40, 46, 47, 48, 57, 69
Schmirler, Sandra, 87
Schutz, Rosemarie, 65
Scott, Barbara Ann, 51–53, 87
Second World War, 49–50, 51, 55
Sequin, Gigi, 66
Shamrocks (basketball, London), 31
Shatto, Cindy, 78
Shedd, Marjory, 70
Shiley, Jean, 48
shinny and double ball, 10
Simpson Kerr, Barbara, 78
Sinclair, Christine, 82
Six Nations Reserve, 46, 69
skating, 21: carnival in Montreal, 6; championships, 25, 33–34, 40–41, 51–52; cost of, 25, 53; at Olympics, 33–34, 48, 67; as respectable, 8–9, 19, 24–25; speed, 40–41, 67–68
skiing, 48, 55, 65, 70, 73, 81
Smith, Bev, 86
Smith, Cecil Eustace, 33–34, 38
Smith, Connie, 31, 32
Smith, Ethel, 36, 88
Smith, Mrs. Sydney, 20
snowshoeing, 7–8, 17, 25
soccer, 11, 19, 79, 81–82, 86
softball, 35, 39–40, 46, 50, 57–58, 69
Soldiers' Wives League (Quebec), 30
Spalding sporting goods, 26
sports car racing, 71
Sports College (Toronto), 56
sports halls of fame, 82, 88
sportswear: ; baseball, 57; basketball, 31; bathing costumes, 8, 28, 41–42; cost of, 15; cycling, 12, 14–15, 17, 18; golf, 22; at the Olympics, 48; pedestrianism, 9; riding habits, 8; softball, 46–47; speed skating, 40; tennis, 20; track and field, 35; Victorian winter, 8
sportswriters, 34, 39, 43–45, 50; as male, 73–75, 88; See also media
squash, 20
Stanhope Cole, Betty, 59–60
Stewart, Helen (Hunt), 65, 78
Stewart, Marlene (Streit), 59, 60–62
Stewart, Mary, 74
Strathcona, Lord, 26
Strike, Hilda, 48, 50
Summerhayes, Violet, 20
Sunohara, Vicky, 81
Sweeny, Violet (Pooley), 22
swimming: 8, 21, 48, 73, 74–75; marathon, 41–42, 61–65, 87; YWCA, 28

Tanner, Elaine, 73, 74–75, 77, 87
television, 57, 62, 77, 81–82, 87–88
tennis, 18–21, 26, 33–34, 43, 54–55, 78
Thacker, Mary Rose, 51–52
Thompson, Jean, 36, 88
Thomson, Mabel (Gordon), 22–23
Thorne, Rosella, 68
tobogganing, 8, 9
Tom Longboat Award, 69

Toronto: basketball, 70; cycling, 13–15, 17–18; golf, 34; Olympics (1928), 36–38; population of single women, 27; skating, 33, 40–41, 52; softball at Sunnyside, 39–40, 46–47; sports run by women, 34–35; YWCA, 28; See also Ontario
Toronto golf clubs, 22, 34
Toronto Ladies Athletic Club, 34–35, 36–37
Toronto softball clubs, 58, 69
track and field; athletes as feminine, 75–77; British Empire Games, 49; international competition, 42; media descriptions, 74; in Olympics, 36–38, 48–49, 87; and reproductive health, 67; run by women, 35; shot put, 56

University Settlement Blacks (volleyball), 70

Vancouver Athletic club, 49
Vancouver Hedlunds (basketball), 58
Van Kiekebelt, Debbie, 76–77, 78
Velma Springstead Trophy, 59, 68
Victorian era, 7–8, 13–14
volleyball, 69–70, 78
volunteers, 84–85

Walasiewicz, Stanislawa (Stella Walsh), 48
walking. See pedestrianism
Warren, L.A., 9
Wheeler, Lucie, 65
Whitall, Beth, 65
Whitehead, Mrs. E.A., 23
Wickenheiser, Haley, 81
Wilson, Jean, 48
Wilson, Ruth, 44
Windsor Collegiate Institute (Ontario), 25–26
Wingerson, Jenny, 75–76
Winnipeg, 13–14, 24, 51, 57
Women's Amateur Athletic Federation of Canada, 35
Women's National Basketball Association (WNBA), 85–86
Women's United Soccer Association, 86
Wurtele, Rhona and Rhoda, 54–55

yoga, 86
Young, Lillas (Lilly), 22
Young Women's Christian Association (YWCA), 27–28, 47
Yukon, 30